I0153419

Fragments
of a
Lotus

Embrace Your Amazing Future
And Let Go of Your Dark Past

Yvonne Sylvester

Fragments of a Lotus: Embrace Your Amazing Future and Let Go of Your Dark Past

© 2018 Yvonne Sylvester All Rights Reserved

Soaring Publications, Middletown, DE

Printed in the United States of America

ISBN: 978-0-692-07231-8

Library of Congress Control Number: 2018902527

No part of this publication may be reproduced, stored in a retrieval system, or transmitted in any form by any means, electronic, mechanical, photocopying, recording, scanning or otherwise, except as permitted under Section 107 or 108 of the 1976 United States Copyright Act, without the prior written permission of the author. Except in the case of brief quotations embodied in critical articles and reviews.

Disclaimer

This book in no way intends to provide therapeutic information or intervention, but rather education and entertainment only. It does not replace the valid and often necessary work of a professional counselor. It is provided with the understanding that the author and publisher in no way are providing legal, financial or psychological advice. The reader, in so doing, agrees to take full responsibility for their well-being and safety in engaging with this material. The author and publisher specifically disclaim any liability for the use or application of the contents of this book.

Some names and identifying details have been changed to protect the privacy of individuals.

Lotus Defined

A symbol of purity of the body, speech, and mind, as while rooted in the mud, its flowers blossom on long stalks as if floating above the muddy waters of attachment and desire.

It is also symbolic of detachment, as drops of water easily slide off its petals.

Contents

Dedication

This book, as well as my life, is dedicated to my protector, my provider, my deliverer, my healer, the Almighty One. Elohim, Yahweh, Jehovah, Adonai, the Creator of heaven and earth, the Lord of Hosts, the LORD of Lords and King of Kings...Abba.

And to my beloved children, Michael, Tyair, Keturah, Nahshon and Majesti. I love you with every fiber of my being. No matter what you face in life, always forgive, let go and press toward the high calling. Situations are meant to teach you and build your character. Remember, it's about your perception; never give up!

Three Cords that Bind...then Me

Who Am I?

Who am I, you ask?

I am a lion who comes off as a lamb.

I am an ocean with waves big enough to drown.

I am a roller coaster of emotions.

I am a hater of ignorant people, liars,

And people who use others for a gain.

I am a lost soul, a naive child.

I am one who has seen enough

That would make most people's skin crawl.

I am me, not you.

I am who I am.

Judging me is only a negative reflection on you.

So who am I, you ask?

I am me...just me.

© Natasha L. Bishop, December 2016

https://www.familyfriendpoems.com/poem/who-am-i-60

Like a tug o' war, I became the tie that bound us together. Two together, then three…four meant me! I was a part of my parents' passion, their love. It's funny how the ties that bind us together can also tear us apart. That's what happened with us. The tie that bound us as a family also tore my mother and my father apart.

I have random thoughts about my early life. Things I remember, though I don't really have a way to categorize them or give them meaning. They are just things I remember, like my great grandma's house smelling of moth balls. My family always coming together to have Sunday dinner. My grandparents having a church in Wilmington and New Jersey. Or that I was put on top of a blasting speaker in my car seat when I was a baby. Early on I spent a lot of time with my godmother and a lady from church I called "Mum." Her real name was Nettie Mae. They were really good to me though, I remember that. My nickname was "Hams," because I had fat thighs. Gratefully that name didn't stick.

One of the best memories I have from early childhood was when Mom, my brother and I made a tape at a studio in Ocean City, Maryland. We sang "The Greatest Love of All." I was four or five then. I lost that tape somewhere along the way. Losing things precious to me would become a theme throughout my life.

I can recall going to a daycare that had blue carpet with yellow, white, green, and red swirls going around on it. There were a lot of cribs and walkers in the room. It was the daycare that I attended when I was a baby. I had to be about a year or so. It's amazing what we can remember, even as babies. Of course, some memories are better than others. I'm just grateful that I can recall such specific detail as that. Having such detailed memories helped me somehow hold on to the things I lost along the way.

Between the ages of six and ten, there were bright spots in our family. Mom and dad had a cleaning business. They started that when I was about seven. Brother and I helped them with the garbage, sweeping and wiping off desks, and got paid an allowance. Mom wasn't much on doing laundry, so she just bought new clothes instead. For a brief moment, it seemed to be golden. We didn't want for anything.

Suddenly, everything changed.

There came a lot of upheaval in my life. Nothing seemed to be very stable. I guess when I look at it, there hadn't been much stability for a while by then. I was coming to learn that my parents weren't to be counted on for much security and safety. Nothing a child could depend on. I had to learn a lot on my own.

Mom was nowhere around when I started menstruation at age nine. My dad was there, and I called for him to please come quickly! That was a strange and confusing time for me. I attended a lot of schools, private and public. I think there were about eight of them before I was in the seventh grade. After school, I went to the West End Neighborhood House and People settlement. It was a welcome break from what was going on at home.

Violence had become commonplace.

I watched Dad beat my cat to death.

We lived in Compton Court, located in Wilmington, Delaware. It was a three-bedroom, two-bathroom townhouse with a semi-finished basement. We had a fish tank in the living room. I wanted a cat, so that's what I got.

One day we were all downstairs in the basement watching television because we couldn't sit on the white furniture in the living room. My cat named Fluffy was sitting there with me. She got up and used the bathroom on the floor instead of going to the litter box. My dad got up and hit her once. She tried to run, and he grabbed her. He hit her again, then twice, then three times and kept hitting her until Fluffy didn't move anymore. I screamed, "Fluffy!!" My dad turned around with such rage in his eyes and yelled at me to go upstairs! I ran up the stairs crying. I just witnessed my dad kill my cat.

I got to my room and closed the door. I laid on my bed, grabbed one of my preemie cabbage patch dolls and cried myself to sleep. I awoke to someone knocking on my door. "Come in," I said as I sat up in bed. The door opened, and I saw that it was my dad. I was mad, infuriated! He said "Skinny" (that's what he called me), I'm sorry, I shouldn't have done that. But you know Fluffy sat right there in front of us and crapped right on the floor. She knew better." I said, "But Dad, you didn't have to kill her." He continued to tell me that he didn't mean to and apologized again. I said, "Where is she?" He said, "I put her in a box until later then I'm going to bury her out front." I slammed my face into my pillow and started to cry some more. My dad went out and closed the door behind him. Moments later, I heard my mother call for us to come and eat dinner. That night my mother made one of my favorite meals: meatloaf, mashed potatoes, and broccoli to try and cheer me up. It worked for the time being. There wasn't much talking at the dinner table that night. Afterwards, I helped my mom clear the table while my brother and dad went out back. Mom and I were in the kitchen and when she heard the door close she turned to me and apologized for what my dad did. She said, "You know he has a tendency for going too far at times." She hugged me and said she would buy me another cat. I nodded my head and said, "Okay. Thank you, Mommy." A few weeks later I came home from school to find a box in my room. I opened it and inside there was a beautiful sleeping kitten. I named her "Shortcake." I said a little prayer over her and took her out of the box, ran downstairs to where my parents were and thanked them for my kitten.

The next few days went smoothly, until one night I heard my parents arguing in their room. My mom was sobbing saying, "Please stop. I'm sorry." He yelled, "Go clean yourself up!" The door opened, and mom came out and went straight to the bathroom. I was still lying in my bed, so I didn't see her face. The next morning, she got us up so we could go to school, and I saw that her eye was black and bruised. With tears in my eyes I said, "Mom…" She looked at me, wiped my eyes and said, "I'm all right,

Baby Dumplings. Go brush your teeth, eat, then get ready for school." I hugged her for a few minutes then got ready. I made my bed, went to brush my teeth, and went downstairs to eat breakfast. My dad was already sitting at the table. I spoke and gave him a hug as usual. After breakfast, I went to get dressed for school.

I went to a private school called New Castle Baptist Academy. It was only one of the six schools that I attended over the course of four years. At one school I attended, if a child was being bad they could use a paddle and whoop the child's butt. One child that was in my class stayed in trouble. The teacher was constantly calling the principal because the principal was the one that was given permission to whoop us with the paddle. My parents didn't give them permission though. If I did something, the principal was to call my parents. I didn't want to know what would happen if my parents were called, so I didn't do anything to get sent to the principal's office. There was one time that I came close.

I was chewing gum in school and I wasn't supposed to. The teacher told me to put the gum on my forehead. I didn't so she gave me a choice: do what she said or be sent to the office. The last thing I wanted was to go to the principal's office. I knew my parents would have a hissy fit if they were called, so I put the gum on my forehead. I had to keep it there for a long while. When I arrived home, I told my mom and she went to the school. She told that teacher off! That teacher never bothered me again! Of course, I didn't chew gum in school anymore either.

One day my brother and I got on the school bus and someone started picking on him. Fights broke out. My brother and I were suspended from the bus for three days. It was a nightmare! We couldn't watch television or leave the house. So, when my parents left, my brother and I went in our parents' room to play on the waterbed. He fell off the bed and hit his knee. I was scared. I thought he was gonna have to go to the hospital and we were going to get in worse trouble. So I touched his knee and prayed the most sincere prayer I could muster. I prayed that his knee would be healed and stop hurting and that he would be better. He said he did feel better afterwards, so we fixed the room up and left it before they got back home.

You know as little kids you try to be sneaky, and some way or another your parents just know when you did something? Well, lo and behold, they knew we had been in there. They never said exactly how they knew, they just knew. We were on punishment for another three days.

We had family gatherings all the time. Either we'd meet at my great grandmother's or my mom's sister's house after church. My great grandmother was my mom's grandmother on her dad's side. Whenever we went to her house, we sat around the table to eat dinner. I can remember the smell of moth balls in every room. By the time we left there, we all smelled of moth balls. There were times that we all would play in my great grandfather's room and he'd fuss at us. My cousins and I would laugh and run out of the house. We thought it was so funny! My grandpop (Mom's dad) lived in New Castle off of Memorial Drive. We'd get together over there and play in the backyard. My grandpa would let us play around him and play with us. He was so loving and fun to be around. I can remember him tickling my cousins and me until we couldn't laugh anymore. Those were the good ole days.

I spent a lot of time with my godmother and family. With her, I had a god sister and two god brothers. Being over there seemed like the main time I had seen a healthy, happy couple, because I sure didn't see it at home.

There are many days that my godmother and family would get together and have a good time. We'd go places, celebrate birthdays, holidays, do gift exchanges, and all kinds of fun things. One of the most memorable times was when she took me to see a Patti LaBelle concert.

The awesome thing about their family is that they're still that way! Not often did I see families getting along, loving on one another and not fighting. Since this is where I spent the majority of my time between the ages of zero to seven, that was vital for me to see. It gave me a perspective that I wasn't even aware of until later in life.

I can recall lying on the counter in the kitchen to get my hair washed by my godmother and I'd hear her bracelets banging together. "Chicka-chicka-chicka" were the sounds the bracelets made as she washed my hair. To this day, I love that sound because it brings back such precious memories.

One day we came home and the lights were off. That's when we went to stay with my uncle who didn't live too far from us. I knew something was going on, I just didn't know what it was. I overheard my uncle telling my parents it wouldn't be wise to move into a bigger place just yet since they just got the business started. They didn't listen. The next thing I knew, we were packing up to move into a bigger place on the other side of town.

My dad, mom, brother and I arrived at our new home and it was nice and big! My brother and I ran in the house to see the rooms so we could claim which room was ours. I got the room that was closest to the steps because that's the room I liked most. The day was busy with getting things moved and put away while my brother and I were playing. There was a knock on the door. My mom went to answer the door and it was the neighbor. She welcomed us to the neighborhood and handed my mom a plate of cookies. They were outside talking and laughing for a while before my mom came back in. She called, "Clay, Thea, come here." I went downstairs to see what my mom wanted. She said, "Go get your shoes on we're going out to get dinner."

There was an elementary school not too far from where we lived, and we rode past there. My mom said, "That's the school you two will be attending. It's not too far from the house, so you two can walk together. Clay you make sure you hold your sister's hand. There aren't any streets to cross, and stay on the sidewalk."

We were walking home from school one day and a dog came out of nowhere and started chasing us. My brother and I ran and then we jumped up on top of a car. A man came out of the house yelling, "Get off my car!" My brother said, "Get that dog first! That dog not about to bite my sister and me!" The owner of the dog called to him from down the street and the dog went running to its owner. We got off the car and ran home to tell our parents. When we got home, my mom and her friend Renee were just pulling up. We told them what happened, and we went to where the dog lived and my mom talked to whoever was there. We went back home, I went to the kitchen to get something to eat before starting my homework. My mom and her friend went out. I must've fallen asleep because when I woke up, I heard arguing. It was my parents because my mom came back drunk.

Things were going good for a little while, no arguing or fighting that I recall. One day my Aunt Carla called from Boston crying to my mom, saying she was in trouble and needed to get away from there. My mom and dad went to my mom's parents' home to let them know what was going on. Upon hearing this, my grandfather told my parents not to go and to let my aunt figure it out on her own. My mom wasn't too thrilled with that because she and her sister were very close. My parents decided they'd talk to my aunt once again and see what else can be done. After a few hours, we went back home and as we were going in the house, the phone was ringing. My mom ran over to the phone and it was the call she'd been waiting for. My aunt and mom talked for quite some time and then it was time for my brother and me to go to bed.

The next morning, my mom said, "We're going to Boston to get my sister." My parents rented a van and packed it with our belongings and food and we were off to a road trip to pick up Aunt Carla. We stayed gone for about a week.

I recall us coming back and things began to get real chaotic! There was a lot of fussing and yelling going on that woke me up many a night. My mom and aunt had gone out getting high and drunk. The fighting got worse than I've ever seen then because my mom started staying out with my aunt. My mom continued going out, staying out, hanging out with various groups. This is when things really started to get messed up. There was one night my mom and aunt tried to come in late and my dad didn't let them in, so they called the cops. The cop came and told my dad he had to leave. My aunt was there for about two weeks, someone came to pick her up and she left. I started missing a lot of school because my mom would go out and take us with her. My dad and mom fought over me a lot because he didn't want me around a lot of people and he found out I wasn't always in school. He came to pick me up and we went back home while my mom and brother stayed over at her friend's house. He started doing my hair or whatever little he did know of, taking me to school and back. It was around that time, when I was nine years old to be exact, that things started to become dysfunctional quickly. Mom and brother came back home and not long after that, we were packing up to move again.

During those years I played the flute at Baltz Elementary and Our Lady of Fatima Private School. I don't recall exactly when that was. I just know I enjoyed it and I was happy. This was also the time of my life that I was in karate, track, tap dancing and singing lessons. Life seemed more "normal" when I was around my godmother and her family. It was nothing like home.

The House that Jack Built

A Grieving Daughter

She told her daughter she hated her and wished she was never born.

She didn't even seem to care that the child's heart was torn.

She blamed the child for all of her heartache and pain.

Did she realize emotional abuse can drive a child insane.

She said her child was the reason she never achieved her dreams.

Those words hurt her child more than to her they may have seemed.

All her daughter wanted was her love and her affection.

But all she ever got was her mother's constant rejection,

Feeling like a lost child with no one to love.

She prayed to be taken away to the heavens above,

Not knowing why she just wasn't good enough.

Why, when she needed gentleness, was she treated so rough.

Wondering why her existence caused her mother so much
pain,
Longing for her mother's love she probably would never
gain.
Wanting her mother to tell her she was a blessing,
That she was not the reason for her mother's stressing.
If there is a little girl out there that feels this way,
Just know you are one of GOD's Angels, and he loves you
more each day.

© Ebony Angel B., August 2008
https://www.familyfriendpoems.com/poem/a-grieving-daughter

JACK = Just As Change Knocks. Between ages 11 and 15, home was a very lonely, isolated place for me. In fact, life really tanked as far as my family goes. At some time around age 11, I started wearing hearing aids on a consistent basis. In addition to all the rest, I was losing my hearing. I wasn't born with hearing loss. I came to find out later that it was due to ear infections. It made everything even more challenging and scary. My dad was the one who helped me get comfortable with having to wear the hearing aids. And yet, the violence continued.

Unfortunately, violence was so common in my house it seemed normal. I've watched my dad beat up my mom a lot. She never fought back. She just took it. She usually ended up with a black eye, busted lip, and bloody nose. One time, Dad broke Mom's tooth. All I could do was cry and try to help her.

I remember one day in the month of May, 1990. We were living at the apartments in Newark after moving out of the house on Greenleaf Road, where we hadn't lived for very long. We lived on the first floor, and that didn't last long either. Mom and Dad had exchanged words and he took the car and left my mom, brother and me at the apartment. He stayed out all night and came back drunk in the early morning. Mom was waiting in the living room for Dad to come back. He tried to open the door but couldn't because the chain was on it. Dad started banging and yelling at Mom for her to open the door, and he tried to bust open the door. Mom was yelling back at him, and all the yelling and banging woke up my brother and me, so we got up and stood in the doorway, watching. As my dad was trying to get in, reaching his hand in the door to remove the chain, Mom reached down to get a big red cup of bleach mixed with Pine-Sol. She pushed his arm out of the door saying she was going to open it, and as soon as his arm was out of the way, she threw some in his face and he screamed. She closed the door, took the chain off and threw the rest of it in his face, then pulled him inside. Dad was hollering saying a bunch of curse words and Mom slammed the door. There was a bat leaned up against the wall. She took that bat and beat him with it. My brother and I took the bat from her. She ran to get the vacuum cleaner and began beating him with that too. My brother and I wrestled that from her, all the while crying, screaming for our mom to please stop. She told us to go get our shoes on and to hurry up as she was reaching to get the car keys from my dad's pocket. She yelled, "Hurry up!" We ran out of the room to the front door; I had one shoe on and the other in my hand. Both of them still cursing one another out, she grabbed our bags and we ran out up the steps and out the building. My mom told us to hurry up and get in the car. She put our bags in the car, we got in and put our seatbelts on. Mom got in, started the car and backed out as I saw Dad coming out of the building. She peeled off as Dad was rubbing his eyes, limping after the car, trying to get to us. She had had enough. She was tired of being beaten on and taking it. On the way to wherever we were going, my mom kept telling us that she loves us and she's sorry that we had to see the fights. "Things are going to get better," she promised. We pulled up to a white house that belonged to a woman named Heather, whom we had never met. Mom turned around and said, "This is where you will be staying for a couple of days." Those couple of days turned into a couple of weeks, into a couple of months, into a couple of years.

No longer did I have a bedroom. I lived in someone's living room. No longer did I have a bed to sleep in. I slept on a couch or on the floor. No longer did I have anything that I had before. It was a stranger's house. All I had fit in the little suitcase I came with. I went from seeing my parents daily to hardly ever, from it being four in a household to more than ten strangers at a time, from eating when I wanted to once a day to catch as catch can, from wearing my own clothes to wearing everyone else's. After she dropped us off, our clothes, toys, my cabbage patch dolls, and pictures were put in storage and never seen again.

I felt hurt, disappointed, alone, unloved, and abandoned. I didn't understand why my parents didn't keep us. I didn't understand how someone could abandon their children. Why not take us to an aunt's, uncle's, cousin's, grandparent's or any other family member's house? Didn't you love me too much to just leave me with anyone? What did I do that was so wrong to make you not want me? I wasn't a bad child. I did what I was told and got good grades. My mind was filled with so many unanswered questions. How did things go from being all right to totally upside down?!

I was finally getting used to being there when my mom showed up, drunk. What now? Unsure if I should be mad or happy that she came back, I hugged her. Instead of hugging me back, she pushed me off her. All I could do was cry. I didn't understand. What did I do to her that was so bad I couldn't get a hug and kiss from my own mother? I ran upstairs and locked myself in the bathroom until she left. I went back downstairs and Heather asked me if I was okay. She apologized that my mom showed up the way she did, hugged me and said that I don't deserve that. Heather thought some candy would cheer me up, so she handed me a dollar to go to the candy store. She certainly was right about that. It did cheer me up. I got my candy and I went to the park afterwards.

Violence became the norm and the expectation for me regarding my parents. Even when I didn't live with them anymore, it's what I expected when I saw them. And they never seemed to disappoint.

There was a time that my parents came to pick me up from the house where I was staying. They had taken me to get something to eat in the city and they were taking me back. Things were going good and we were all laughing and having a good time. All of a sudden, my dad turned to my mom and punched her in the face. He drove off the main street toward a back road. POW! He punched her again. I was screaming at the top of my lungs, "Stop, Dad! Stop! Please stop hitting my mom!" My mom opened the door to jump out while the car was still moving. He grabbed her so she couldn't jump out, stopped the car, and then *pushed* her out. No one was around so I couldn't scream for help. He told her he would kill her and got out of the car. I was on the same side as her, so I jumped out and kneeled by my mother. He yelled at me to move! I screamed back, "No!" He raised his hand to hit me but turned around instead and told me to get in the car. I did. He got in too, started the car and began to pull off, leaving my mom on the ground bleeding. With tears streaming down my face I pleaded, "Dad, please don't leave my mom. That's my mother over there. If you leave her, you'll have to leave me too, 'cause I'm not going without her." He stopped and opened the door for my mom to get in. She was getting in and as she was reaching up to grab the handle to pull herself up, I saw that she had a black eye, busted lip and bloody nose. Instantly, I started crying again, reaching and grabbing for her.

I felt so helpless. There was nothing I could do to stop the attacks, nothing I could do to keep my mom safe. But then, there wasn't much I could do to keep myself safe from her either.

It was time to go back to school and my mom called and told me to get a ride to the Hilton. I called my godfather, Wesley, and asked him to take me. I arrived there and saw that my mom had bought me a bunch of clothes and school supplies. I was so excited! Of course, I was happy that I finally got something new. I was picking up everything off the bed to put it in the bags when my mom said, "Baby Dumplings, I'll bring it to you so you don't have to carry everything by yourself." I said okay, hugged her, told her I loved her and left. Days went by and she didn't come. She didn't call. And she didn't bring my clothes. I called her numerous times and got no answer. When she finally did answer, she told me she took everything back to the store. I couldn't believe it. I was crushed. Here I was, still wearing other people's clothing because I didn't have anything of my own to wear. Everything she bought me, she took back to the store. It didn't make sense to me. Why would she do something so mean to me?

I started meeting people around the neighborhood. They knew my situation. Some of them got together and donated clothes. There was one woman that went out boosting so that I had clothes. Kids by then were making fun of me because I wore the same thing all the time. It was all I had. I have to admit, though, having new clothes didn't make living in the house with so many people any easier.

One time I was lying on the floor trying to sleep. There were multiple people around. I felt a hand on my thigh. I was terrified, so I didn't say anything. Next thing I know, he started violating me. I didn't know what to do because I've never been touched like that. I thought if I said something, no one would believe me, or I'd be thrown out. I kept my mouth shut. I had to leave, but where would

I go? He then said, "Don't say anything to anyone," and that's when I knew who it was. I was still a virgin, so what did I know, other than that it was wrong? All I could do was lie there and pray. That was the beginning of the end of my innocence.

I didn't realize that the violation was going to trickle down to so many other areas of my life. I started smoking Kools and drinking whatever I got my hands on at the age of 12, and smoking marijuana by age 13. I got caught smoking a cigarette at school. My teacher covered for me. Through all of this, I still got good grades. I skipped most Mondays and was bright enough to make up the work on my own.

The next day I looked for my brother. I hadn't seen him in some time. When I found him, I went to stay where he was. At least I had him now.

Life started looking up then. I didn't have a care in the world. No one picked on me and we all looked out for one another. We were a family. I had a curfew but snuck out with the eldest daughter whenever everyone else was sleeping. Yeah, we got busted quite a few times, sneaking in the house. The mom started threatening to put me out, but I didn't care. She saw that it didn't mean anything to me, so she started whooping my butt along with her daughter. It did little good…ha! At this house is where I started getting new clothes. I was happy to just have one new outfit that I could call my own!

On my twelfth birthday my godfather came to see me. Of course, I was happy. I went to the Boys and Girls Club just about daily. He came there to pick me up and took me to McDonald's to get something to eat. He said that he wanted to take me somewhere to meet someone. I didn't think anything of it. We drove for a little bit before we reached our destination. We got out and when he knocked on the door, a woman answered and greeted him saying, "Hey, Dad." He turned to me and said, "Thea, this is your sister Leah. Leah, this is your sister Thea." I looked at her like "Yeah, whatever, nice to meet you, god sister." In my mind, I didn't need a god sister; I had one already. We stayed there for a little while and left. As we were going back to Rosehill, I said, "Wesley, why did you call her my sister?" He said, "Well, umm. Well, umm. Your mother and I were supposed to sit you down and talk with you about this." Still not understanding what he was talking about, I said, "Wesley, what do you mean? What were you and my mom supposed to talk to me about?" By then we were back at the Boys and Girls Club. He turned the car off and looked at me. He said, "Thea, you are my daughter." I looked at him and said, "Yes, I know. I'm your god daughter." He said, "No, you're my biological daughter." All I could do was sit still, looking straight ahead. I was so confused. I said, "What? Wait. How?? But...wait. I thought Sonny was my dad." He said, "No, he's not. He adopted you." He told me how my mom was pregnant before she got with Sonny. He said he wasn't sure whether I was his or not until people went back and told him I look just like him. He didn't want to mess up my mom's marriage, so he became my godfather. I turned to him with tears in my eyes and said, "So wait. You are my dad and you see what I'm going through. Why didn't I come live with you? You know my mom dropped my brother and me off at a stranger's house. Why didn't you take me???" That's when the excuses came. I wiped my face and said, "That's okay. You don't have to take me. I'll be all right where I am." I gave him a hug and kiss, told him I love him and to have a good night. I went back into the Boys and Girls Club and headed for the bathroom. I locked myself in the stall and bawled! I was hurt, upset, disappointed, confused and angry that no one wanted me.

The feeling of being unloved filled me and surfaced once again.

It was sometime later that my mom came around telling me that I was moving back with her. I wasn't too thrilled about it, yet I went. When I got there, I noticed that my mom and her boyfriend had been living there for a while. My mom showed me around and took me to my bedroom. Happy that I finally had a bed to sleep in after a couple years of sleeping on a couch and the floor, I laid down and went to sleep. I awoke later that evening only to find that I was home alone. I went to the kitchen to get something to eat and there was nothing there except a gallon of ice cream. I looked around for a phone so that I could call my mom and didn't find one. It was after 5 o'clock, so calling Wesley was out. Since I knew I wasn't going to be eating, I went back upstairs and went to sleep. The next morning my mom still wasn't there. I tried to go back to sleep but couldn't. I got up and dressed, then went outside to see if I could find someone's car in the driveway, so I could use their phone. That's when I saw a childhood friend across the street. "Niecey," I called. She looked at me and said, "Who's that?" I said, "It's Thea," and started walking toward her. We talked for a while before she invited me in. Her parents were making lunch and said I could stay if I wanted to. Of course, I stayed, I was starved. I used their phone to call my mom only to find that she wasn't where I thought she'd be, which was at the club. Niecey's parents invited me to stay for dinner as well and again, I accepted. Afterwards I went home, and my mom still wasn't there. I saw her and her boyfriend the next morning when I woke up.

I attended a school for the deaf. My hearing never improved, and I still wore the hearing aids. I met a dorm counselor named Jefferson. I found out that he lived down the street from me and we became close. He was like my caretaker when my mother wasn't anywhere to be found. He made sure I ate, did my homework, and encouraged me to continue in school. At that time, he was the main person that looked after me, and I was grateful.

After a while I got tired of always being home alone and being away from my friends and the people I knew, so I went back to stay with the family where I had the most fun. By now nothing mattered to me. Things were all about what I wanted, getting drunk, smoking, and hanging out. Why not? I mean, no one cared, so why should I? My mom, biological dad, and a stepdad didn't check on me or make me a priority, so I was left to do whatever I wanted. In fact, Mom told me she hated me from the bottom of her heart and called me every name but a child of God. So, I got back to doing whatever I wanted to do.

In New Castle, I had more access to everyone that I knew and I didn't have to be alone. I had abandonment issues, but I didn't know that's what it was at the time. When I returned, I had been missed, and I was loved on from every direction. That love meant passing the bottle or the smoke.

One thing that I made sure of was that I went to school. I wanted to learn. I was hungry to learn. I wanted to be better than I was. I wanted to get out of the area that I was in. At that time, I couldn't do anything except deal with the situation I was in and enjoy it while I could. Basically, I made the best of whatever circumstances I could. I was 13. What did I know about raising myself?

Abandoned, Lost and Alone

I Wish I Wasn't Alone

Once when I was little
I was happy and carefree.
I used to run around laughing
Until it was time for tea.

I used to play games
And smile all the time.
I used to feel on top of the world.
I used to feel fine.

It's amazing how things change
When people let you down.
And how that once happy face
Turns into a solemn frown.

You search and search
For someone who cares,
Anyone who understands,
Anyone who dares.

FRAGMENTS OF A LOTUS

Loneliness, it hurts.
It kills you deep inside.
It makes you feel empty.
It stops you in your stride.

You cry yourself to sleep,
Hugging your pillow tight,
Wishing for someone
To hold you through the night.

Once when I was little
I was happy and carefree.
Now my life's full of sadness,
Pain and misery.

Once when I was little
I was never on my own.
But now I pray at night
"I wish I wasn't alone."

© Jo, June 2011
https://www.familyfriendpoems.com/poem/loneliness-hurts-i-wish-i-wasnt-alone

I was at my mother's friend Meka's house when my dad, Sonny, came to pick me up. He wanted us to get a fresh start and that fresh start was supposed to be in Virginia with his side of the family. I was happy because I really wanted to be with at least one of my parents on a regular basis, around someone I knew loved me. We left and were having a good ole time laughing, talking, and singing. I was on my way to another state to meet family members I didn't know I had and to start fresh. I was finally going to be with my dad consistently. We got on I-95 South to go. My dad then turns to me and says, "I have to ask your mother something. I really need to find out what the hell her problem is leaving her children, especially my daughter, with some damn no-good people." I said, "Dad it's all right. It doesn't matter because I'm not there anymore." He got off at the next exit, sped through the green light and made a U-turn to go where my mother was. I said, "Dad, let's just go. We don't have to go back there. Please, Dad, turn back around and go to Virginia so I can meet my other family." He ignored my pleas and continued driving. He went to one place where he knew she would be and she wasn't there. He went to where she lived, and he didn't see her car there either. I said, "Dad, let's just go. It doesn't matter why she did what she did anymore. We are together, and we can leave." He still didn't respond to what I said. He went back to Meka's place and spotted the brown Cadillac Seville which was my mother's car. He got to the stop sign and told me to get out. I started crying and said I didn't want to. He was only going to make matters worse. He said, "Oh Skinny, I'm not going to leave you. I just need you to get out the car and stand on the sidewalk." I begged him to please just let us go. He turned to me and yelled, "Thea get out of the damn car right now!" Crying, I got out of the car and closed the door. He started revving up the engine and leaned out the window and yelled, "Bon, Bon!" No one came to the window, so he yelled again, "You b****! I bet you'll come to the window now!" He accelerated and went right for her car, BAM! He slammed into my mother's car. "Daddy, stop it!" I yelled at the top of my lungs. He didn't even look at me. People started looking out their apartment windows to see what that loud noise was as others were coming outside. My mother and Meka looked out the window. Mom furiously yelled, "Sonny, what the hell is your problem?!" He backed up and revved the engine once again. He said, "Bring your ass downstairs!" She told him no, so he slammed into her car again. Then he backed up and sped off. I watched as his car peeled away. I stood there until his car was out of sight. Right after, the cops pulled up and my mom came out from the apartment building.

I left them all standing there. I went upstairs, tired, alone, confused and frustrated, to say the least. Sitting on the couch, I was mad as ever that my dad left me, which meant I wouldn't be leaving all the drama. Here I was again, stuck in the middle of a chaotic situation created by my father and mother. Meka and my mom came back in the house and she started cussing me out, saying that's why she doesn't like me because of stuff like this. I looked at her and said, "But Mom, I had nothing to do with that." She started telling me how that was my fault and I shouldn't have ever left with him. She went to the refrigerator, grabbed a beer and started drinking. *This is going to be a long day*, I thought.

I was so right. More of their friends came over and it was time for them to party. Smoke of every kind and music filled the air. There was beer, liquor and coolers all over the table and kitchen counters. I didn't have anywhere to go and no means to leave, so I went outside to sit on the steps. I needed to get away from all the noise and men.

After a few hours, one of Meka's sons came outside and sat next to me. "Are you okay?" he asked. I looked at him, shook my head, got up and walked away. I walked and kept walking. By the time I got tired it was well after 11 p.m. I had walked way across town where I knew my brother would be, or at least the door would be open as it always was.

In the house, I found my brother sitting on the couch watching TV, drinking beer and smoking a cigarette. I looked at him and said, "You won't believe what happened." Slurring he said, "Come on, wait Thea. I'm watching something." Exasperated and disappointed, I sat on the other couch and fell fast asleep. The next morning, I awoke to tell him, but he was gone. I got up, showered and dressed to get ready for another day. My stomach started growling, reminding me that I hadn't eaten in over 24 hours. I went to the kitchen, got a piece of bread, balled it up and ate it. I heard someone coming and looked to see who it was. It was Olivia, the mother of that house. She asked when I got there and I told her after 11 the night before. She asked where I had been and I told her I was at Meka's and what happened while I was there. She pulled out a chair and told me to sit down while she cooked breakfast and we started talking. A couple of hours passed while we talked. Afterwards, I decided to go to the Boys and Girls Club to burn off some steam.

Wandering...

My mom was living in Hamilton Park and I went to live with her again. It wasn't too far from the people that I was always around, and I could still ride the same bus. By this time, I was 14 and I had my own bed and room again. The first night there, I slept like a baby. The second night was when things started.

There were strange men coming in and out of the house, so every time I came out of my room, I was met by some men sitting at the table smoking crack or coolies, doing heroin, and shooting up. I grabbed the house phone and went back to my room. I stuffed a sheet or blanket underneath my door so I couldn't smell it. That went on every single day. In the fridge there was nothing but baking soda and in the freezer was only ice cream. I called my uncle and godmother a good number of times and asked them to bring me food because there wasn't anything there to eat. Their first question was always, "Where is your mother?" My response was either she was in the bed asleep or who knows? They'd come bring me food and money, then leave. I didn't always want to call and bother them, so a lot of times I went without. I went to one of my friends' houses to eat whenever I was invited. One friend, Trish, knew my situation, so she'd invite me over to eat with her and her family about twice a week.

There was this one evening the doorbell rang. When I answered, Kim, my mom's friend, was standing there crying. I told her to come in and called for my mom. She came out from her room and asked Kim why she was crying. They went in my mom's room and closed the door. I went into my room, closed the door and got on the phone. A little while later I heard them out in the living room talking, so I opened my door to be nosey. Mom and Kim were sitting in front of a statue talking to it. I came out of my room and asked who they were talking to. They ignored me. Mom lit a candle and said whatever it was she said and put some stuff in the lap of the statue. It was freaking me out, so I went back in the room and closed my door. A few minutes later I heard the door close. I went back out to the living room and called for them. No one answered so I locked the door. Several hours passed and they came back laughing and talking. Kim said something to the effect of, "That grave site really helped, I know things will be better and now I know what to do." I got chills all over and closed my door. I was absolutely terrified. I didn't want to stay there knowing they were communicating with only-God-knows-what. I was so scared, sleep didn't cross my mind that night.

The next day I got up to go to school and went to see the counselor. Being able to talk with her on a regular basis helped me to keep my sanity. I shed so many tears in that office. I didn't like my life, and often wished I could turn back the hands of time. When she asked to what time I wish I could turn it back, I really couldn't answer. If I turned it back to when I was a baby, I was barely with my own mother. If it was turned back to when I was a child, I still had to see all the fighting between my parents. Honestly there was no escaping, so I had no choice but to keep moving forward. I sat there and cried because I didn't want this life. Why did I have to go through this? Why couldn't I have the life that I dreamed of having: a two-parent home, with peace, love, and unity? After I finished my session, I went back to class, and throughout the day I pondered the situation. I had one friend there that I talked to about everything. I saw her and we got to talking, and she was able to cheer me up. I could laugh and smile again that day. Interestingly, it wasn't too often that I didn't laugh or smile. I believe that's what got me through a lot of my days and helped me keep my sanity. I'm a firm believer that laugher is good for the soul, as it has kept me many a day.

Even at a young age there were times that I would be in the house alone. There was no supervision, no support and no care. I'd have to call other people to bring me something to eat. Sometimes I could find someone and sometimes I couldn't. Most times I called on my godmother. She was available and would help me no matter the time of day. I love her dearly. She is who I looked to for guidance and direction. I am forever grateful for her and my god sister.

Together again…or so I thought

My mother came to me and told me she's taking me to the doctor because I was sleeping way too much. I went to bed early and when I came home from school I took a nap. The puppy I had was always up under me too, which was very different, and it brought back memories for her. Mom sat me down and told me a story. She began telling me that she was over at her aunt's house one day and the puppy that my aunt has never went to anyone. When the puppy, which was a poodle, saw my mom, he followed her and stuck up under her. My great aunt asked my mom if something was wrong. "Why is Bubble following you?" My great aunt said, "I'm calling your father." "I didn't think anything of it," my mom said. "Daddy came to pick me up and took me to the doctors because something wasn't right."

The first thing he asked them to do was a pregnancy test. Sure enough, it was positive and when they did an ultrasound they found out I was seven months along. "So, because of how Princess is hanging around you and the way you're sleeping I know you're pregnant. And if you are, you're getting an abortion." I laughed and told her I'm not doing that.

The next day she took me to Planned Parenthood. They told her that her suspicions were confirmed. I was pregnant. She looked at me and said, "You're 14 and don't need a baby." She started telling me that I need to get rid of it while it's still early. I told her that I'm not going to do that and I'm keeping my child no matter what. We had a big argument about it that day. Later she cooked, and we sat down to eat. She said I'm telling your father. I got scared then, but I still stuck to keeping my child. That was the last time we discussed that topic.

A few days later, I heard my puppy, Princess, barking. I went to the door to see who she was barking at and saw my dad opening the gate to walk up the stairs. I ran to give him a hug. He looked at me and said, "Is it true?" I put my head down and said, "Yes, it's true, Dad. I am pregnant." He shook his head and hugged me again. I told him Mommy was trying to make me get an abortion. He said emphatically, "No! Don't do that! Where is she anyway?" I told him she was out with Dana. He started talking so I sat down on the step and listened to him. We sat there talking for quite some time and when my mom didn't come, he asked me if I had eaten yet. When I said I hadn't, he said, "Okay. Let me go get us something to eat. I'll be right back." He hugged me and left. I sat outside waiting for him. Hours passed and he didn't come back. I went in the house. A few minutes later, my mom walked in the door handing me a bag. It was chicken tenders and French fries. That had to be the best chicken tenders and fries ever, I thought, even though I didn't see my dad again.

A couple of months passed. I went over to my sister's house. I was supposed to be there for one day and ended up staying for a few weeks. That was the longest that I've ever been around my sister, and I enjoyed every moment. She was the sister that I always wanted, but never knew I had. My biological dad, Wesley, came around and that's when I told him I was pregnant. His eyes got big and he said, "Oh yeah, I figured with your stomach looking like you ate a watermelon." I laughed and told him that's because I had just finished eating. I told him that I was having a blast with my sister, nephews and niece and wish I had known them a lot sooner because that's time I can't ever get back.

I asked when I would meet my other siblings. We talked and shared a heartfelt moment, then he apologized for waiting so long to tell me who he was and about my siblings. I felt very disconnected from him. I felt he didn't think I was good enough to be his child. It didn't make sense to me why a man would allow his child to call another man "Dad," and call him by his first name. I called him by his first name for years and he didn't say anything or even try to correct me. I told him that I didn't intentionally call him by his first name once I found out

47

who he was, it just seemed weird to me. My sister was calling him "Dad" while I called him "Wesley." It was very confusing to me as to who I was, since I was a late comer. I didn't allow that to bother me though. I kept it moving. I had questions that needed to be answered, but I was going to enjoy the moment and not dwell on what couldn't be changed. What I did understand is that I didn't want to be an outsider on both sides of my family. That was too much. I built a relationship with my sister and her children. And it started feeling normal for once.

It was time to return to school, so I went back to where my mom lived. I was about six months pregnant by then, and although they didn't condone teen pregnancy, they let me stay. I was one of the students that the staff loved, so they decided to have a surprise baby shower. Well they also knew about my living situation and wanted to help in every way possible. I went to school until my doctor put me on bed rest and set me up with a visiting nurse. I had one teacher that lived close to me, so she would gather all my work from my teachers and bring it over, then take it back on a weekly basis. I was grateful for that because even though I was pregnant, I didn't want to be behind in my work. I had to finish school no matter what. One day I was sitting in the living room and my visiting nurse showed up. I was surprised because she usually came to see me on Tuesdays and Thursdays, and it was a Wednesday. I let her in and asked if everything was all right. She said she was in the area and felt she needed to come over to check on me. I told her I was fine and felt fine. She said she wanted to check my blood pressure. When she checked it, she said she had to check it again on the other side. I let her check it again. She said, "Let's move you to the couch so I can take it while you're lying down." I moved to the couch and she checked it again for the third time. Then she said, "I have to call this in. Your blood pressure is very high. I'm concerned." She got on the phone and her supervisor told her that I needed to get to the hospital immediately. She turned to look at me and asked where my mother was. I told her she's out, but I could try to reach her. She told me if my mother wasn't there by a certain time to call her or her supervisor because I needed to get to the hospital. I assured her that I'd keep her posted and walked her to the door. After she left, I called around looking for my mom, leaving messages with every number I called. I couldn't reach her, so I called my nurse to let her know I couldn't find her.

Just when I was about to say good-bye, my mother and her boyfriend pulled up. I told her that she didn't have to call an ambulance now. I went outside and told my mom what the nurse said and went to get my bag for the hospital stay. When we arrived at the hospital, they already had a room ready for me, saying that Ms. Nita, my nurse, called to inform them of the situation. I called my closest friends and a few other people to let them know it was about that time. A good amount of people showed up. They all couldn't come back to my room, so they had to wait in the waiting area. I was surprised, to say the least, but happy that so many people cared. It amazed me.

My mom called family members and told them what was happening. I don't know all of everything that was going on because they weren't really telling me much. My mom took over. All I remember is them saying my baby or I could die, and they had to induce me. I was talking to my mom when they started an intravenous line on me. The next thing I knew I was waking up to visitors. Within an hour of waking up, my mom was screaming and, well, my son was born. He was healthy, which was what mattered to me.

I arrived back to my mom's house a few days later with my son and found some baby things in the living room. I saw a card on one of the gifts and opened it. The gifts were from those at my school congratulating me on a successful delivery and healthy son. I waited until the weekday to call and thank them. Marie, who was my counselor, asked what I had. I told her what the four things were, and she was shocked! She said, "What do you mean that's all you see?!" I said, "That's what was here when I came home." She began to tell me that there was a whole truck full of stuff that was brought to my house. I asked what it was, and she said she'd get with everyone and make a list of the purchases. I started crying and said my mom must have taken the things back to the store because she was good for that. Marie continuously apologized and said she's going to see what could be done. I found out what was purchased and that my mom took it all back to the store.

I was so furious that I didn't have anything to say to my mom. It took me a couple of days to tell her that I knew what she did. She was high again as always and told me whatever is in her house belongs to her and she could do whatever she wanted to do with it. If I didn't like it, I could get out! That wasn't unusual; she was always telling me that.

There wasn't any company over to the house for a few weeks, which was surprising because there was always something going on there. Before long, the drinking, smoking, and various strangers running in and out started again. I couldn't go out of the room without walking into a cloud of smoke or seeing a new face amongst the crowd. The area where they were doing all their business was right by the room where my son and I slept. I stuffed blankets under the door so the smoke wouldn't come in the room where we were. It worked for a little bit, but then my son started coughing all the time. I dealt with that for a couple more weeks until I had somewhere for us to go. Then I left. I went to my son's grandparents' house and stayed there for a couple of months. His grandmother, great grandmother and grandpop were a big help to me in so many ways. His great grandmother especially taught me a lot about babies that I didn't know, and I will forever be grateful to her for that. We had a lot of talks and she helped me with my baby, her first great grandson.

I had to get back to school, so I called my counselor to see what could be done. I had to get some papers signed, but my mom and dad were nowhere to be found. I discovered my mom had left to go to Oklahoma without telling me. When I found out, I let my counselor know and they started a child protective case and assigned me a worker named Ms. Dot. I couldn't stay where I was anymore. My son's great grandmother had fallen ill, so my son and I moved in with my biological dad Wesley, in Newark. By this time, it was the year 1995. My son was a few months old. He was a baby that cried a lot, so because of that I spent countless time on the phone with my godmother trying to figure out what was wrong with him and what to do to calm him. She asked me to describe what he was doing. I told her he was crying like something was wrong. He was clenching his fists, pulling up his legs and wouldn't take his bottle. She told me to feel his stomach to see if it was tight. It was. She asked if he had gas. He did. After explaining all the symptoms to my godmother, she told me he had colic. That was a nightmare in and of itself.

He kept me up most of the night for about a week straight. Things got back to normal with his sleeping pattern after he was better. My dad, Wesley, started fussing about him crying, keeping him up at night and how I had to do something about it. I apologized to him and assured him I was doing all that I knew to do. Wesley started hinting how he wasn't used to being around teens or babies and something had to change. I called my case worker, Ms. Dot to let her know what Wesley was saying and how I believed he had been hinting about us moving. She wanted to get me and my son in a group home, so we could stop bouncing all around from place to place.

She went to my school to get my birth certificate, but they didn't have it. She had to get it from vital statistics. She called me and asked me what my name was. "What do you mean?" I asked. She said, "There isn't any record of you being born here." I told her that as far as I knew I was born here, so I'm not sure why they can't find it. She told me that she asked them to double check to make sure my name wasn't spelled wrong. The lady told her that I wasn't in the system. She said, "Listen, I really don't know what is going on, but ask some family members what your mom named you." I asked her what my school records say. She said to just find out what I can and call her back by the end of the week. I got off the phone and I was confused more than ever. I called Wesley at his job and asked him what my name is. He said, "What do you mean?" I told him what had transpired, and he said, "You were definitely born here. You were born at Wilmington hospital, that I know for sure." I said, "But did she tell you what she named me?" There was a long pause. I said, "Hello?" He said, "I'm here. Umm, no she didn't tell me." I told him I'd see him when he got home. I waited until the evening and called my god-mom. I told her what happened, and she was like, "That is your name. That's what she named you in the hospital." Then she said, "No, wait, your last name is Burns." I said, "What?!" She said, "Yes, when you were born your last name was Burns, so maybe she didn't change it legally." I was beside myself. I said, "So wait, I've been using Sylvester and that's not my last name?" She said, "Did you ask your mother?" I said, "I don't have a way to reach her. I heard that she is in Oklahoma." She said, "What? When did she go there?" I said, "I'm not sure. I have to call my aunt or grandpop and find out who she's with there. I think she's with my aunt, but I'm not sure. Aunt Marie, I really don't know what's going on and I'm more confused than I've ever been."

So, who am I? Here it is, I'm a teenage mom, with a child and don't even know what my name is. So, I have someone else's name on my son's birth certificate? I was so beside myself, I just broke down and cried. After I got off the phone and got myself together, I started calling around. I called Sonny, the dad that raised me and asked him. He said, "I named you Althea." I said, "Yeah, that's what I thought too, but apparently that's not my name." He asked what I meant, so I told him what my case worker found out. He started snapping then because he didn't know either. He said, "That woman is always doing something. What the hell did your mother do?" I said, "Dad, I don't know, but I wish I did." I said, "So why don't we know that and why isn't my name on my school records?" He said he wasn't sure and that it was my mother's doing. "Where is she at anyway?" I said, "I heard she went to Oklahoma, but I'm not sure how to get in touch with her yet. I'll call Aunt Dana to see if she knows." We continued to talk about a lot of things, then said our goodbyes. It was in the early evening and my biological dad, Wesley, came in from work. He asked me if I found out yet and I told him no, but I was going to call my aunt after dinner.

After everything was done, I put my son down for bed and called my aunt. I asked her the same question I'd been asking all week. She told me the same thing everyone else told me. My first name is Althea. I sighed and felt that no one knows what my name is and that was such a shame! I asked her if she had the number to where my mother was. She gave it to me. We said we love one another and hung up. I was debating whether I wanted to call my mother that night or if I had had enough for the day. I decided to call it a night; my head was spinning and hurting from all that confusion. I didn't want to think about it anymore, I just wanted to relax, watch TV, laugh and forget about what I was experiencing. I went to the freezer, got some vanilla ice cream, and sat down to watch some television.

The next afternoon, I called the number my Aunt Dana gave me. My Aunt Joyce answered the phone and said that my mom wasn't there; she was out. I asked if she would let my mom know I called and gave her my number. Several hours later the phone rang. It was my mom.

We talked for a while before I could muster up the nerve to finally ask her what my name is. She asked me what I meant. I told her what happened when my case worker tried to get my birth certificate. She said, "That's because Althea is your middle name, not your first!" I said, "So, what's my first name then?" She said, "You're named after me." I asked her why she was just telling me that. She went into this long, drawn-out reason about how I didn't want to write my name the way she told me to and I refused to be called anything other than Althea. I said to her, "So Mom, if that's the case, why does the school know me as Althea? Why didn't my dad know my first name wasn't Althea?" She started yelling at me and cussing me out, so I said, "I'm hanging up" and did so. Yes, I cried again because my feelings were hurt.

Who does that to their own child? Why would a mother want to confuse their child when they're responsible for caring, nurturing, protecting, and loving on them? It was after 4 p.m. by the time I got myself together, so I had to wait to call my case worker to tell her what my name is. The next day, I called and let Ms. Dot know what I had found out the day before. She went to vital statistics and got my birth certificate. Of course, I was happy that I knew the truth. I called my dad and told him what I found out. He asked me for my mom's number, which I gave to him, and we got off the phone.

My biological dad, Wesley, came home and said he wanted to talk to me. He brought dinner home and we sat down to eat. Then he dropped a bomb. He said, "Your mom called me today and I think it's best that you move in with her, so she can help you with the baby." I said, "What?! How is she supposed to do that, when she can't even care for me? Besides that, she's in Tulsa, and I don't want to go there." Mom was in Oklahoma with her sister trying to get herself together. They both decided they wanted me to move to Oklahoma with my mom. He told me that I had to leave his place in a week even if I didn't go to Tulsa, because he couldn't deal with the baby. When he got paid, he'd purchase me a ticket. I sat there angry, thinking about how there were so many changes going on in my life. It was too much to wrap my head around it all.

Of course, I was hurt, disappointed, upset and frustrated thinking *This is my dad, how can he do this knowing what I've been through?* That didn't seem to matter to him; he just didn't want to have a crying baby any longer. Over the next few days I packed up our belongings and planned to move to Tulsa. I let my case worker know so I could get my birth certificate before I left the state. I went back to my son's great-grandparents' house for a week, so they could spend time with him before we left. Then I called Ms. Dot and she came to pick me and my son up and took us to the bus station. That bus ride was every bit of two-and-a-half days.

When I arrived, my mother and aunt were at the bus station to get us. My dad and brother came to Oklahoma as well. We stayed with my Auntie in her efficiency for a while. My mom and dad were both working and saving up so we could get a place of our own.

Things started coming together. We were going to be a family again. We started going back to church and there wasn't no arguing or fighting, which was very surprising. They weren't doing any drinking or drugs; they were both clean. I couldn't believe it. Little did I know, this was going to be one of the biggest hiccups I've had to face with them, being a teenage mom.

I found a program that I could attend that would allow me to finish school. It would allow me to go for four months and I'd be done. I felt I had both my aunts, uncle, my mom and dad, which was more than enough support. I didn't want to leave my son for that long. I called and spoke to my aunt and she assured me that they'd be there to help with my son, so I could get my education. I felt relieved and thought, *What better time to go than now?* I filled out the application and was waiting to be accepted. I received a phone call a few weeks later and they informed me that I wasn't accepted. I wanted to know why. The lady told me that she wasn't supposed to tell me, but the reason was because of my hearing. I thanked her and let my mom know the reason. We talked, and I called back to the office. I spoke to the person in charge and they had changed their minds. They let me know I could start in a couple months. I was ecstatic and ran to tell my parents. Once they found out, we celebrated. I figured I'd try to get a job, so I could get a little money before leaving. A few days later I was on my way to Arby's when I saw my mom's friend. We started talking and I let her know the good news. It was then that she dropped the bomb on me! She informed me that if I was to leave and attend the program, my mom was going to take my son and return to Delaware with him. She was going to go to the courthouse to file a petition to get custody of my son and say that I abandoned him. She said then she'd get custody of my son because I wouldn't be around or know what was happening. I felt like someone had just stabbed me in my heart! *Back to the same old games*, I thought. What in the world was I going to do now?! At that moment I decided I'd have to find another means to get my diploma. How was I going to finish school and move ahead if every time I turn around my own mother is trying to hurt me?! I went home and talked to my dad about it, and that's when I found out he was leaving.

Later that week, my mom and I were sitting at the glass dining room table, talking. She mentioned she'd be moving back to Delaware and she'd keep my son while I went to school. *You were planning this the whole time*, I thought. I let her know that I wouldn't be staying in Oklahoma while she takes my nine-month-old son back to Delaware. She was holding her grandson, and at that time she got mad at tossed him across the glass table, and I caught him. We got in an argument over that and I left the house.

I went to the neighbors' house around the corner and told them what had happened, between sobs. They got the number for social services for me and I called. I spent hours on the phone with them. I found out I could become an emancipated minor and get my own place. The place would be in Broken Arrow, OK, which wasn't too far from Tulsa. An appointment was made for me to be seen by a worker the next day. I thanked the neighbors and left to go back home. When I returned, the lights were off. I went to my room, closed the door and got ready for the next day.

The next morning, we got up at the crack of dawn and I got us dressed so we could take the bus. I knew where the bus stop was, but I didn't know which bus to take. I had failed to ask that, I was so distraught. I was just standing there, and I began to pray. Not even ten minutes later, my friend's mom was riding by and she saw me. She turned around and asked what I was doing. I told her, and she said to get in the car. I folded my son's stroller up and got in the car. I told her what had happened the night before and she apologized that I was going through that. She said she'd take me. We arrived at the social service building and I spoke to a worker. We were there for three hours. The caseworker reiterated all that they told me over the phone and let me know the process of becoming an emancipated minor. It sounded good, but I was 16 years old, what did I know about living alone with a baby in a whole new town with no one that I knew? Things were kind of that way, but at least if I returned to Delaware, I'd know people there. Thinking how things would be terrified me, so I didn't do it.

When I returned from Oklahoma, I went back to stay in New Castle. One thing I always knew, if I needed a place to lay my head, they were there for me. I stayed there for some time with my son. By this time my son was about a year old. I took my son to visit with his dad one day and let him stay there for a few hours. I returned to pick him up and the great-grandmother told me my son wasn't there. I asked her where he was, and she wasn't trying to tell me. I called the house to speak with the dad, but he didn't come to the phone, so I left to go to the police station. The cop told me I had to go to court to get my son back. I returned to the grandparents' home and that's when the great-grandmother let me know that my mom had him. I had no idea where my mom was, so I called to inform my case worker, so she would know what was going on. I went all over, to where I thought she'd be and that wasn't successful. It was later on that evening when I found out where she was. I went there with a few people to get my son, and that's when all hell broke loose, and the cops were called. She told the cops that I didn't have custody of my son and I was a drug addict. I informed the cop that I have a case worker and he could contact her to find out the facts of this story. He told us all to go to the police station where things would be sorted out. The worker showed up after a while and explained the situation to the officer. The officer came over to us all and told my mom that she had to return my son to me. If she wanted visitation, she'd have to take me and the dad to court. She gave my son back to me and said, "Well since you're keeping him, he's not keeping the sneakers I bought," and took the sneakers off his feet. I laughed and said, "That's fine, he has sneakers already." We left before anything else happened. Several weeks later, I received a certified letter from the court. It was my mom taking me to court for custody of my son. In that petition, she wrote all that she was, but turned it around on me. I went to file a response to the petition, while also filing to be removed from her custody. It wasn't long before the court date came, and I was awarded sole custody as well as removed from her and my dad's custody. It was a long, drawn-out battle, but I never gave up. I maintained my faith and joy throughout the process. I thank God that He kept me.

Black Sheep

Growing up, I was around my aunts, uncles, cousins, grandparents, and great-grandparents. We had a lot of family functions and we went to the family church where my great-grandmother was the Pastor. Just about every Sunday, we got together and had dinner. After my parents split, being around my family was history. Once my mother and father didn't show up, neither did anyone else. That part of my life was snatched away. I didn't understand why things were happening the way they were. I just knew that things were upside down on every angle. I was lost and alone, not knowing what to do or even who to trust. No longer did I have the family that I was surrounded by at one time. No longer did I have my brother that I grew up with, because we drifted apart. He went one way and I went another. I'd see him and say hi, but conversations didn't really go any further than that.

I can recall one particular situation in November of 1995. My uncle came to where I was looking for my mother because my grandmother fell ill. I told him that I hadn't seen or heard from her in days. I asked him if it was bad and he said, "Yes, so she needs to get to New Jersey a.s.a.p." I told him I wasn't sure when I'd see her and asked if I could ride with him to go see my grandmother, as that may be the last time I saw her. He told me no and to wait for my mother to take me. I said, "I don't know when I'm going to see my mom again. Please take me to see Mother." He said, "I told you to wait for your mother," and he left. I didn't see my mom that day or the next, but I patiently waited. A few days after, the phone rang. It was one of my family members calling to tell me that I needed to sit down. From the tone in her voice I knew something was wrong. That is the day I found out my grandmother passed. I was angry at my uncle and my mother because neither of them picked me up or gave me the chance to see her again for the last time to say goodbye. Later I found out that everyone else was there, and that made me angrier. I felt like an outcast, the black sheep in my family. I started putting a wall up because I was tired of being ignored and feeling like I didn't matter. I didn't want to hear anything that my aunts or uncles said because I knew it wasn't genuine. I started to look at how they treated me, not what they said. One thing my mother always told me is to watch how folks treat you more so than what they say. "Actions speak louder than words, baby dumplings," she would say. My kin folks would be together, but I wouldn't know anything about it.

My family knew that my mother dropped my brother and me off over a non-relative's home, yet they did nothing to intervene. My brother and I were good kids that enjoyed going to school and being part of extracurricular activities. They knew we were young and scared, yet not one of them came to our rescue.

I didn't understand what I had done wrong, or why no one wanted me. We weren't bad children; we were smart and went to private schools and was on the honor roll, so what was the problem? When I asked, they said, "Well you know how your mother is." What does that even mean? That was the response mostly everyone gave.

What I had to realize is, the reason no one came to my rescue is because this was my cross to bear. I had to learn how to deal with things. This was to be my testimony, my story, my patience, my trust, my confidence, my cry out to God in the time of trouble, my humbling experience. See had someone come to my rescue, I wouldn't be able to weather the storms. My story wouldn't be able to help others. I realized that this is all for the Glory of God. Because of the storm, I've learned to trust Him; I know how to lean on Him more. I know how to pray, travail, and cry out. I didn't know that then, but I know that now. Back then, I was angry at my parents and my family. I felt they didn't think I was good enough to be around them. I felt alone and cast out like the black sheep left without tools for the battle. But God is the One that sustained me and for that, I'm grateful.

Unforgiveness Will Not Have Me in Bondage!

I don't hold anything against my mom or dads for not being there when I needed them most.

I have forgiven them.

Why should I hold on to all that I've been through? I can't think of one valid reason. Some have said "Well, they didn't protect you as they should've." Others have said, "They abandoned you at such a young age." Yeah, that all may be true. Yet that is all forgivable.

What I know is that people do what they know to do or what they care to do. Should I live my life in pity because I didn't have what I feel I should've had growing up? No, why waste my time on that when I can make a better life for myself now? I can learn from what I've endured, turn it around and do better for my own children, which I have. Why allow anyone, regardless of who they are, parent, brother, sister, aunt, uncle, cousin, or friend, dictate my future and livelihood? Why not forgive and stop carrying those people around with you everywhere you go? That's like carrying a weight and being anchored, ready to sink your own ship. One being anchored can go nowhere. They're stabilized, stuck, and unable to move. Being anchored by unforgiving is being anchored to your past. That is what I refuse to be. I refuse to allow anyone to have me anchored by not forgiving them.

Being unforgiving affects you emotionally, physically, mentally, spiritually, and financially. Why hold on to what a person has done or said to you when you can free yourself of that? Unforgiving is like a cancer that eats you from the inside out. It kills slowly, and it can be cured with as little as your making up your mind and deciding to forgive.

When we forgive, we give up the right to pay a person back, so to speak. God said vengeance is His. Another way to put it is, what goes around comes around. No one can escape that. The golden rule is to do unto people as you'd want done to you. Some may find that hard to do, but look at the bigger picture. Why tie yourself up in a big web of unforgiveness, bitterness, anger, hatred and resentment? Your freedom is much more valuable than holding a grudge toward someone who did you wrong.

There are those that don't even know you feel the way you do because nothing was expressed between you about how you feel. Then there are those that didn't do things intentionally to hurt you. Then of course there are those that hurt you purposefully. One thing that I've learned over the years is that what a person puts out is how they truly feel *about themselves*. Don't allow a person to cause you to be tied up spiritually, physically, emotionally, financially, or mentally. All of that also affects a person's health.

I can say for me, I always look at the brighter side of things. When my parents made the choices they made, I now know they did what they knew to do. It took me some time to understand that. Of course, as a teenager I just thought my parents didn't want me, so I turned to others and the streets to get the love I was missing. Then I became a teenage mom thinking I could get the love from my child. I was terribly wrong there because I had to give him love. The love I had within me, I gave to him, and that gave me even more reason to push forth and not hold on to what I've experienced. I learned to let it be my teacher and to do better than what was done to me. I vowed to always be there, no matter what.

Had I kept unforgiveness in my heart, I would've been messed up, and only God knows what would've happened. Instead I chose to forgive, cry for my healing, laugh and smile no matter what. That is something that's worked for me. I had to be the one that made that decision, though. No one could make it for me. I know I didn't want to have any sort of bitterness or hatred in my heart. I chose to love people instead, even when it wasn't returned, because that's what was in my heart to do.

My mom passed in 2014, and I can say freely and with a clear conscious that I stuck by her until the very end. I saw her a day before she passed, hugged, kissed her, and let her know I love her. When she left this earth, she knew without a shadow of a doubt that I had forgiven her. Even she couldn't understand why I didn't hold any anger toward her. There were times she'd cry and tell me she was sorry, and I'd stop her and tell her that I forgave her many years ago and she needs to forgive herself. We had that conversation many, many times. She didn't know how to forgive herself and she allowed it to eat her from the inside, which happens to so many people.

There are times we do things that we either know we shouldn't have done, or we regret doing afterward, and we hold on to it. Forgiving ourselves is major, and the first step we must take toward healing. There are times that I'd do things and forgiving myself was the hardest thing. It's funny because I could forgive others at the drop of a hat, yet I'd beat myself up over what I did to myself, knowing that I knew better. It took me a while to realize I was even doing that, until someone brought it to my attention. I had to reflect and repent and start the process of forgiving myself. It was then that I realized that things start with me and then go outward. Forgiving isn't something that we should take lightly. We're poisoning ourselves when we hold unforgiveness in our heart. We're creating a negative vibe when we don't forgive, and that is felt everywhere we go, and more importantly, it's felt within our very being.

Some may ask, "How can I forgive this person for doing this or that person for doing that?" The key is deciding to do it. Deciding to free yourself of their hold. Deciding to let go and move forward in greatness. Once you decide to let go of the people who have hurt you, whether intentionally or unintentionally, you can start to be a better you. You'll see things more clearly. You'll want more, and the weight will be lifted off your shoulders for you to fly, for you to bloom, blossom, and soar in your very gifts and calling. See, when you forgive there is something that happens in your soul. You may not be able to explain it fully; you'll just know things are different. You'll be able to see that person you forgave and won't look at them side-eyed or cringe when they're in your presence. You'll be able to look at them and not feel any anger or hatred toward them. Forgiveness is the key to the beginning of deliverance and healing in your mind, body, and soul. Once you forgive, the atmosphere will even start to shift around you. You start to bring people of positivity around you instead of negativity.

No longer do I view my situation as, "Why me?" I reminisce and thank God for bringing me through with my sanity still intact. I thank God for allowing me to be humbled through all those experiences and to see the glass as half full instead of half empty. I view it and say, "But God! I made it! I'm making it!"

I was able to give my children a better upbringing than I had. I was able to keep them all together no matter what came our way, and I didn't give up. I stayed in shelters, motels, a group home and from pillar to post, yet

I kept us together and didn't give up. As crazy as it may sound, I'm grateful for what I've been through. I look at it and say I'm glad it was me that went through it so that my children didn't have to. It stopped with me and a new beginning was birthed because I chose to forgive and let go.

You cleanse your heart, your mind, and your spirit of toxins. Now although we can't see the toxins, they are there. That's just like we can't see the wind, yet we feel it when it blows. Unforgiveness is like clogging your very own being with toxins and expecting it to cause the other person harm. It's like squeezing glass and expecting the other person to bleed. When you put toxins in your body, you're harming yourself. When you squeeze glass, you're going to feel it and bleed, not the person you're holding a grudge against. Why give a person that much power over your life? You must be the healthiest, most empowered you, and you can do that by forgiving yourself and anyone who's caused you ill feelings toward them.

Unforgiveness causes unwanted, unnecessary stress. It causes people to relieve pain by drinking and doing drugs. People act out in different ways for different reasons. For instance, I started drinking because I didn't want to think about my parents leaving me with strangers, and I was out there fending for myself at such a young age. That was my way of coping with it. I knew that I shouldn't have, yet I did it anyway because it felt good at the time and since my parents didn't care, then why should I? I was angry as a teen because I felt my mom should've left her husband, not us. My brother and I weren't causing the problem; we just watched as it happened, ran, hid, or jumped in to stop the fight. As I got older, I realized it had nothing to do with her not loving us. She did what she thought was best, and that's my late mother's truth. It may sound unrealistic, yet that was her perspective and her way of helping us all. I knew that I didn't want my child or children to ever feel the way that I did and that there had to be a better meaning and way of loving them. I love my mother and showed her until the day she left this earth. She was a brilliant, fun, and funny woman that got caught up in the things that carried her away from facing reality. Unfortunately, that happens to so many others. I only wish I had more time to get to know who she was.

I chose to forgive my biological dad for seeing me go through all this yet choosing to do nothing. He just sat back and watched. Yes, he'd bring me food and money, but it wasn't the same as giving me stability, especially when he had it to give. He knew I was his daughter, yet he washed his hands of the responsibility of me in many ways. I didn't really know him, and who knows, maybe he felt the same and didn't want children living with him. Regardless of what his truth was, I had to forgive him to be a better me. Once I did that, I saw him in a different light.

I chose to forgive my stepdad for putting our family through the many sleepless nights and tears shed because of him beating on my mother. I forgave him for the times I had to watch it and scream at the top of my lungs for him to stop. He taught me to never tolerate a man putting his hands on me. I learned what not to do from going through and seeing what he did.

And during that time, my faith grew. This is a scripture that really spoke to my heart when I needed most to know that the Lord was near:

Psalm 103:8-12

The LORD is compassionate and gracious,
slow to anger, abounding in love.
9 He will not always accuse,
nor will he harbor his anger forever;

10 he does not treat us as our sins deserve

or repay us according to our iniquities.

11 For as high as the heavens are above the earth,

so great is his love for those who fear him;

12 as far as the east is from the west,

so far has he removed our transgressions from us.

This is the prayer that helped me let go of any bitterness, anger and unforgiveness. I pray that it helps you as well:

> Dear Gracious Heavenly Father, I come to you in the name of Jesus repenting of every deed and spoken word that has gone against Your will. Lord I ask that you search my heart and show me if I harbor any unforgiveness toward anyone. Bring them to my remembrance so that I can forgive and release them of any wrongdoing they've done toward me. I desire to be free mentally, physically, spiritually, emotionally, and financially. So right now, I forgive, release <say the names of the people>, and let them go from whatever they've done to me. Deliver me from the spirit of unforgiveness and heal me from the hurts that

they've caused me. Create in me a clean heart, O God, and renew a right spirit within me. Thank You Lord for my breakthrough. I decree and declare I'm free from all anger, bitterness, grudges, and resentment, for who the Son sets free is free indeed. I thank You Father for hearing and answering my prayer. Amen.

So, you see, the choice is really ours and ours alone. We have the power to decide if we're going to hold on to people or let them go and be free. No one can decide that for us. Once we get of age, we determine where we go in life, not the one that hurt, abused or mistreated us. We could've had an uprooting childhood, the best childhood, middle childhood syndrome, or an abusive childhood. It matters not the circumstance. Although we do learn what we see, we can also choose to change the course which we decide to follow. It's all in our mindset. It's our perspective that we must change and that can be done by first forgiving yourself and others so that you can be free. Free from the abusive thoughts, free from the abandonment, free from the negativity. We have to learn to be our best selves in spite of what has happened in our past.

Don't allow your past to determine your future. Only use that as a guide to know what not to do or what to do better. There's a reason the rear-view mirror is smaller than the windshield. We're supposed to look ahead to our future of success, forgiveness, fulfillment, growth and change. My aunt used to tell me as a teenager/young adult, "Change isn't change until you change." It took me a while to get that, but once I grasped that concept, I lived by it. It means, in order for things to be different, I have to want change. It doesn't matter whether you change the people you hang with, the city you live in or the abusive relationship you're in. In order for change to happen, it must first start with us.

Start the change by forgiving so that you can set yourself free and not have to carry the weight of those on your shoulders any longer and be anchored to them. Set yourself free, sister! Set yourself free, brother! You can do it; you got this! Take your freedom back and live life to the fullest! Don't allow people to steal your joy. The world didn't give it, so don't allow the world to take it away.

I can say that the things that helped me get through were prayer and reading the Word. There are several songs that reminded me that God is omnipresent, and He has me. I look back and thank God that even though I was alone a lot, I made it to my destinations without being attacked or kidnapped. I must've played those songs thousands of times. One was "My Help" by Sis Jackie Gouche Farris. The others are on the album "Mercy" by the late Andrae Crouch – "God Still Loves Me" and "The Lord is My Light" are two songs in particular that spoke to my heart.

I didn't allow my past to define my future, and I still don't. I look at everything and say it's not for me but for others. There is a purpose for all that happens. Who would've known that I would be sharing my story with the world? I count it all joy and know that all is well because no matter what, I choose to free myself and not allow unforgiveness to have me in bondage!

I Chose. I Forgave.

Just Let It Go

In time,
Things come
Things go

With love,
Leaves fall
Leaves grow

The morals of life,
Have no beginning
Though it seems the trials
That we face,
Have no ending

Words said to hurt,
With thoughts made to
Kill

The only way to express
a pain that I feel

Just let it go...

© Durwin Davis, November 2011
https://www.familyfriendpoems.com/poem/just-let-it-go

I realized not forgiving not only stressed me out, it also made me someone I'm not. Although I'd be laughing and smiling on the outside, I was hurting on the inside. I was suppressing the emotions that I felt, not realizing it was only making me angry. I had so many queries that I've never gotten the answers to and will never get the answers to. I had to come to grips that some things aren't going to be answered. I had to move on.

There is a lot of research about the effects of parental substance abuse on children and the effects of domestic violence on children. I get it now why so many of my questions would never be answered. The adults in my life couldn't be accountable to answer them. Not only that, but while they were living their lives and doing what they do, their behavior was having a direct effect on me.

There were things I could never change and things that I could never understand.

According to the research, my experience in that environment was fairly common. My mother was not able to provide for me when she was around. She was not physically, emotionally or mentally capable of providing for my basic needs. There was often no food in the house to speak of. Equally as often I had no clothes to wear. Whether or not I was aware of it, I probably suffered from PTSD as well.

There is not much research regarding the dual exposure of children to domestic violence and parental substance abuse. What is known is that there are behaviors that children exhibit that are the direct response to violence and substance abuse exposure. It explains why I made some of the decisions I made.

Consider these statistics from the Department of Human Services:

- 3.3 million-10 million children are at risk of exposure to family violence.
- 80-90% of these children are aware of the violence.

- Children in homes with domestic violence are abused or neglected at a rate 15 times higher than the national average.

- In 60-75% of families where a woman is battered, the children are battered as well.

- 63% of youthful murderers kill their mother's abuser.

- Children older than five or six have a tendency to identify with the abuser and lose respect for the victim.

- The most serious cases of child abuse resulting in emergency room treatment are often "extensions of the battering rampages launched against the child's mother, with 70% of the serious injuries to children and 89% of the fatal injuries inflicted by men" (Governor's Commission on Domestic Violence, 1995).

- 50% of the time police respond to domestic violence calls, children are present.

- 71% of victims using a domestic violence shelter bring their children.

- The United States Conference of Mayors found nationally 75% of all homeless women and children are on the streets because of violence in the home.

- 67% of state child welfare workers said that AOD-involved families (alcohol and other drugs) are "much more likely" to re-enter the child welfare system over a five-year period compared to non AOD-involved families.

- Alcohol is abused by more than 15 million American adults.

- Children whose parents abuse substances are almost three times more likely to be abused and four times more likely to be neglected.

- At least 40 million children live in homes where the primary caretaker is addicted to alcohol or other drugs.

- Up to 675,000 children per year suffer serious abuse or neglect as a result of that substance abuse.

- Two out of three cases of "child abuse" have a co-occurrence of domestic violence and substance abuse.

- *The best way to protect children is to support their mothers' efforts to attain safety and sobriety.*

Adolescents (ages 12 – 17)

All of the previously mentioned plus:

- Feelings of guilt.
- Delinquent behavior.
- Running away.
- Alcohol/drug use.
- Eating disorders (need to control).
- Among sexually active teens, males are more likely to be sexual offenders and females are more likely to be sexually assaulted.
- Re-enacting relationships – based on control/ dominance and not respect or equality.
- Parental caretaking at personal cost.

http://www.dhs.state.il.us/page.aspx?item=38483

What chance did I have?

The ones who were supposed to care for me, were receiving my care. In addition to those statistics, there are others that speak to my own substance use, truancy, molestation, sexual activity, teen pregnancy, and the like. It appears that my acting out was not unusual considering the environment in which I was raised.

I decided to view things differently about my life and what I've experienced. I really don't know what my parents went through or even how they were raised. I also don't know all that they've seen or the views they had. We are a product of our environment, yet when we are old enough we are responsible for the decisions that we make. An example may not have been given, which would make it hard to see past what we are surrounded by. I knew there was better than what I've experienced because I've seen it. I had to realize that I was in shackles because of how I was being raised and because I had unforgiveness in my heart against my parents and family.

I thought I forgave them until my mother and I were talking one day and I broke down crying. In that moment is when I chose to free myself. I forgave my mother for everything she'd ever done. I told her I had to forgive her for my own sanity and move on. No longer would I hold on to the things of the past that hurt me. I was only harming myself physically, emotionally, mentally, and financially. I'm the one that was in bondage and was harboring anger. There was such a relief of peace that came over me.

I realized that I'm the one that holds the key to my release and happiness, not anyone else. I had to want my freedom and peace bad enough, and I did. I started forgiving and releasing all those from my past that have hurt me. I took back my strength by letting go of those that I have carried for so long. Those I knew I hurt, I asked them to forgive me as well. All that I was doing to forgive was for me to be free. It had absolutely nothing to do with anyone else.

In all that forgiving and freeing myself from their hold, I failed to forgive the person that mattered most: me. I failed to allow myself to feel exactly what was going on with me. I failed to forgive myself for not saying anything about being molested when I was a child. I failed to forgive myself for allowing others to use me. I failed to look at myself in the mirror and love on me. I needed to forgive me for wronging myself. My deliverance came in forgiving. My healing came in forgiveness. I knew that I didn't just go through this for me, but for others as well. I had to love on me and I was too busy pleasing others and forgot about myself.

Yes, I had joy because I knew the world didn't give it to me, so the world couldn't take it from me. Yet what about my happiness and peace? I was so constantly looking for others to appease and fulfill me that I didn't see that it's me that's responsible for that. No one is responsible for my happiness but me. No one is responsible for my success but me. No one is responsible for making choices for me. I had to do that.

I had to take my life back and it started within by seeing what I allowed, forgiving myself and forging ahead. It wasn't that I didn't know how; I just didn't practice it. I was so busy trying to wear all types of hats that I failed to wear the self-love and forgiveness hat at all times. Does that mean I have to just allow people to do whatever they want to me over and over again? No. That simply means I know what I will and will not tolerate, and if someone cannot respect my boundaries, I move on. Not everyone deserves a seat at your table. You have to know that.

Getting to the core of the issues isn't an easy task, yet the outcome is so rewarding. Being able to love you past your flaws and soaring into your greatness is priceless. Whatever we feel about ourselves always shows and comes out in actions, words or energy. Frank Outlaw is credited with saying "our thoughts become words; our words become actions; our actions become habits; our habits become character; and our character becomes our destiny" (paraphrasing). In other words, watch what you think. If you constantly dwell on what someone did to make you angry and how you don't forgive them, will never forgive them for what they did, it will come out in your words, actions, habits, and character and become your destiny.

Forgiveness means getting delivered and healed from that thing or those people and moving on to a better you. One may say they can't do it all in one day. That may be true. Things happened over a period of time and it may take a period of time to recover. That's fine. So take it day by day.

We can't run or hide from our true selves. It comes out whether you want it to or not. We cannot lie to ourselves, thinking that forgiveness isn't necessary, because it is. It's a daily task and the moment we think we can't conquer it is the moment we have lied to ourselves. We can conquer whatever we set our mind to. It's a willingness to want to forgive. No one can make you forgive. Yet, I can tell you that you're only going to give yourself freedom by doing so. Sometimes it takes days, weeks, months and even years to dig deep enough. It depends on how deep that well may go. It's a lifelong journey.

You will forever be changing, growing and learning if, and only if, that's what you decide to do. You decide what you want for you. I did because I knew it was a necessity for me to move forward in my thoughts, actions, habits, character and destiny. I knew that I wanted better for me and my children. It's my hope that you will face whatever has been holding you back from forgiving and choose to forgive for your freedom. It's my hope that you will overcome your challenges, forgive yourself and love on you so that you can soar.

My intention in writing this book is to provide you with the tools, techniques and insight that you need to successfully forgive anyone of anything. That's the beauty of forgiveness. Once you have the basics, you can use it time and time again. You've just heard my story. I'll share the process that helped me forgive my parents and everyone else that hurt me in my youth. If I can forgive, I know you can!

Forgiveness: The Why and How To

This Pain

This pain that I feel cuts through me like steel.

It's like an open wound that just won't heal.

They say that time is the key that turns the lock and sets you free,

But why, God? Why is this happening to me?

Through the wind he whispers to me:

Be patient, my child, and you will see.

The lessons learned will set you free.

Feel my love and serenity,

And I will guide you through this troubled sea.

Fill your heart with love and forgiveness,

And it is then you will find that golden key

That turns the lock and sets you free.

© Theresa M. Montoya, October 2016

https://www.familyfriendpoems.com/poem/this-pain-8

Why Forgive? After All, We Were the Ones Hurt!

Hurt, betrayal and suffering on some level are all a part of life. No one living will escape it. Our feelings will be hurt by those who say they love us and by the stranger on the street. Just keep reading if you doubt what I'm telling you. In fact, chances are, since you've gotten this far in this book, you already know the truth of these words.

You also may be wondering by this time, why you have to forgive. You probably feel like you are owed an apology by someone. They are the perpetrators of your pain. They are the source of your disappointment and despair. Don't they then have to come to the table and acknowledge the impact of their actions? Aren't they accountable for how they've hurt you? Why do they get off Scott-free? "It looks to me like they haven't had to do anything in this," you might be lamenting. "I'm the only one hurt here. It seems like they haven't lost anything. It looks like they are getting over on me. I'm the only one suffering. They have prospered on my back. I'm the one who has been abused, abandoned, neglected and rejected." Sound familiar? There's a lot of resentment, grief and anger in those words.

Here's the truth. All that you believe is true, is. You probably are due an apology. You probably have been abused. You probably have been abandoned. You probably have been neglected. You probably have been rejected. And they may actually be doing well at your expense.

Does any of that make a difference now? It does, but only in what you decide to do with it. There is a scripture that says we should honor our father and our mother so that we would have a long life. It does not, however, say anything about our parents being honorable. The responsibility lands squarely on our backs to regard them with honor, notwithstanding their character or behavior. The same is true here. Who they are and what they've done bears no witness to your responsibility to forgive.

I've mentioned it before: Forgiveness is a decision. So why is it a decision we should make...to forgive? To answer that, I want to show you the effects of unforgiveness on the person who has suffered the harm.

The source of unforgiveness is relentless anger or frustration. It may also include unyielding hatred and even violence. Physically, mentally and emotionally, it contains the root of bitterness expressed through a heightened state of distress. It is prolonged rigidity of thought. Unforgiveness, according to psychologists, is a chronic stress response. That means that unforgiveness holds the person harmed confined to a mental, emotional, never-ending stressful mindset. Another way to put it is that it is a place of mental, emotional, self-imposed bondage. The mental effects of unforgiveness are:

- depression, including suicidal thoughts
- chronic stress
- fatigue
- insomnia
- paranoid thoughts and the development of a paranoid personality
- eating disorders including anorexia and bulimia
- communication issues
- trust issues
- relationship issues
- anger
- fear
- intimacy issues
- lack of self control
- bitterness

- self-destructive behaviors
- substance abuse
- bullying
- domestic violence
- co-dependency

Did you see yourself in that list somewhere? It is by no means an exhaustive list. Of course, there are other thoughts and behaviors that could have their basis in unforgiveness. These are merely the most prominent ones. The tragedy is that too often, as Shakespeare said, "The eye seeth not itself." Frequently, it's hard to see the truth about ourselves. The knee-jerk reaction is to "excus-a-lize" our own behavior. After all, we have good reason for doing the things we do and making the decisions we make. The unforgiving mindset is quick to explain how right we are about how we feel and how righteous we are to feel that way. The thing is, it's not hard to find people to agree with us in our righteousness. So many of us have been through similar situations that their unforgiveness agrees with our unforgiveness. It's like the blind leading the blind, and we both fall into a ditch.

It's a dangerous thing to be in the place where we are not able to see ourselves. Or not able to receive wisdom that is shared with us from wise counsel. Or surrounded by those who support us in our continued bondage. I'm not sure I want to hear from someone who is in the same trap I am and who doesn't seem to want to be made free from it. I wanted out.

It is no secret that there are negative physical effects of stress on the body. For years this has been studied and researched. The connection that we need to see here is the one between unforgiveness and the body. Yep. There are physical repercussions for not forgiving. They are probably connections that you haven't even considered prior to this moment. I need you to hear it and to take it very seriously. This truly represents the concept of drinking poison and expecting the other person to die. Unforgiveness is dangerous to our health.

Researchers have determined that there is an indelible connection and interrelatedness between the mind and body. Changes in the body are the result of this link. Consider this: there are physical, chemical reactions to mental and emotional stressors. We see an impending danger and adrenaline is released for us to respond appropriately. We enter the fight or flight state immediately, depending on our natural proclivities. Either we prepare to run, or we prepare to defend ourselves. That physical reaction triggers additional mental and physical reactions. Muscles tighten. Heart rate increases. Cortisol, the stress hormone, is released by the adrenal glands.

Now this is important. Please pay careful attention. The situation of chronic, unending stress, such as is evident in the state of unforgiveness, leads to the problem of adrenal fatigue. Adrenal fatigue is a physical condition that affects many areas of our lives. It is the body's response to chronic stress. The adrenal glands, which help us manage stress, become overtaxed, tired and spent. They can no longer effectively help us with stress. They become the victim of our stress. When they are exhausted, they cause more problems than they can heal. Here are some of the symptoms of adrenal fatigue:

- Anxiety
- Overwhelm and the inability to handle stress
- Struggle getting up in the morning
- Asthma
- Lack of muscle tone due to loss of strength
- Allergies
- Extreme use of stimulants, including caffeine addiction

- Dark circles under the eyes
- Extraordinary fatigue and weariness
- Dizziness
- Lines in the fingertips
- Depression
- Food cravings, especially for salty foods
- Low blood sugar
- Dry skin
- Urination frequency
- Respiratory issues
- Sleeplessness and insomnia
- Late night spikes in energy, high energy levels when one should be sleeping
- Joint swelling and pain
- Low blood pressure
- Compromised immune system, weak immunity
- Low libido or sex drive
- Back pain, especially low back, neck and shoulder
- Poor circulation, especially in the fingertips
- Weight gain and inability to lose weight

That's a pretty extensive list, isn't it? Remember, this is the result of on-going, unresolved stress, like that within unforgiveness. An interesting note is that according to cancer research, a great many cancer patients have issues with unforgiveness and that unforgiveness is considered a "disease" by the medical community. Many cancer treatment centers are now adding forgiveness therapy to their cancer treatment regimen with success. In his book, *The Forgiveness Project*, Dr. Michael Barry reports that 61% of all cancer patients have forgiveness issues. Of that 61%, half of them have severe forgiveness issues. These same issues with forgiving may actually even keep the patients from accepting treatment in the first place. The link between your health and unforgiveness is very real and extremely potent.

The flip side of these costs would be the benefits of forgiving. Here are a few of those:

- Fewer anxiety symptoms
- Stress reduction
- Fewer respiratory and breathing issues
- More sound, restful sleep
- More sustainable energy levels
- Lower blood pressure
- Less anger and hostility
- Enhanced anger-management skills
- Lower heart rate

- Improved psychological health
- Lower risk of alcohol or substance abuse
- Fewer depression symptoms
- Increased mental stamina, focus and attention
- Reduction of chronic pain symptoms and experience
- Improved spiritual health
- Better blood sugar regulation
- More friendships
- Healthier relationships

You may notice that the benefits of forgiving are almost the exact opposite of the costs of unforgiveness. That makes sense, given the far-reaching nature of forgiveness.

In short, the reason we need to choose to forgive is so that we can be healthy, spirit, mind and body. There is too much at stake for us to hold on to unforgiveness a moment longer. I also need you to notice something about the physical and mental effects of stress: they have nothing to do with the person that harmed us. Everything listed above impacts us, not them. We are the ones who can't sleep. We are the ones with joint pain. We are the ones drinking caffeine all day long and then struggling to get up in the morning. We are the ones with respiratory complaints and a weakened immune system. We are the ones, not them (unless they have their own unforgiveness issues).

These are the reasons we must choose to forgive. We must make that choice so that we are no longer in mental, emotional bondage but also so that our health may be maximized. We must make the choice because it is in our best interest and highest good to do so.

Is Forgiveness Possible? You Don't Know My Pain

Now that you know the reasons you must make the choice to forgive, next you have to assess the landscape. There may be certain blocks to forgiveness that you must account for and give attention to in order to successfully forgive. Unless these boundaries are overcome, your forgiveness efforts could be stymied and ineffective.

The first block to forgiveness is unreadiness. Very simply put, you are not ready to let go of the offense. You're not ready to be over the hurt and pain. You remain in the self-righteous place of how you've been done wrong. Your emotional turmoil is unresolved. It delays forgiveness and derails your healing. It's like being stuck in a loop you can't get out of. Maybe you're compelled to rehearse and repeat the wrong. And to compound the matter, you may even find that you ruminate on not just the most immediate issue, but on every hurt you've ever been through. Suddenly you are fixated on how unfair life is and it just gets bigger and bigger in your head and your heart. When this happens, it becomes really challenging to shift your perspective away from the hurt. No amount of encouragement or "look on the bright side" suggestions can move you from that square. After all, you're right about how you've been mistreated.

The fact is, you're just not ready to forgive. And you won't be ready until you're ready. As the old adage goes, "Time heals all wounds." Chances are, the more you practice the insult or harm, the less likely you will be ready to forgive. If it continues to be the focus of your thoughts and it still feels as painfully sharp as if it just happened, you may need more time to pass before you're ready to let it go. Time not only serves to put space between the initial offense and the present, it also gives the offender time to establish a new track record of trust. Why is that important? Any time you can step back from the incident and process it in a larger framework or perspective helps to put it in a more acceptable context. As time passes it is possible for the intensity of the event to subside. Thus, the intensity of the pain also subsides. It then becomes easier to forgive and let it go.

Another block to forgiveness is the need to avoid embarrassment. In the vernacular, it is the need to not be "made a fool of." This concern is intrinsically tied to the need to protect one's reputation and public persona. It threatens one's self concept. The fear of being perceived as a fool, a doormat or a sucker. This is also a concern with feeling public and internal shame.

The concept of shame is different from that of guilt. Guilt says that you did something wrong. It can be corrected. The behavior can be changed or improved. Shame says that there is something wrong with you; the essence of you is wrong. To go a step further, shame says the wrong of you cannot be corrected. Ever. So, then it follows that if there is public shame, it can never be overcome. Once you are considered a fool, that becomes your identity. Nothing can ever change that. No matter what wonderful things you do behind the foolish decision or behavior, a label has already been ascribed from which you will never be dissociated.

The fear is that forgiving, then, may cause the one harmed to appear weak, further damaging their reputation. It becomes almost a badge of honor to hold on to the offense. The anger seems to take on a life of its own with an added dash of indignation and resentment. It feeds the self-righteousness of being harmed.

It's not unusual for this fear to surface under these conditions. Even those of us who are not public figures have these concerns. We begin to wonder what people are thinking of us. Who knows what happened? How far has this gone? Especially with social media being what it is, it can be difficult to believe the whole world doesn't know about the situation.

Has the perpetrator told everyone and made me look like a punk? Have they been bragging about what they did to me? These thoughts make it harder to let go of the offense. And because we don't want to look weak, vulnerable, pathetic, or gullible, we hold on to the anger. We may even plan some kind of retaliation, so we can feel justified or vindicated. Stop it. This only contributes to our inability or lack of desire to let go of the offense, and thus the inability to forgive.

This reluctance to let go of the grudge contributes to some sense of personal control as well. On some level there is a sense of power for the one harmed if they hold on to the hurt. It may be the only way they can feel empowered in the situation. If we find ourselves with this approach to being hurt, it may be an indication that we need to strengthen our self-worth or self-concept.

Holding on to the hurt and anger could result in plans to retaliate. Research suggests that retaliation may really only feel good in the moment. What we think is that we will feel fulfilled. We think that seeing the other person suffer the same pain we have will make us feel better. Psychological evidence is to the contrary. Even in as few as ten minutes after the retaliation, the mood slipped and the person started feeling worse.

Counselors who work with clients that have been abused, abandoned, neglected, or betrayed have found that ruminating persistently on retaliation fantasies results in intensified feelings of shame, anxiety and remorse. These very thoughts take up psychological and emotional resources that could have been used toward developing healthy coping mechanisms. And the acting out of these fantasies leaves the person worse off than when they suffered the initial hurt.

The people most likely to seek revenge or retaliation are those who feel their self-worth or value has been weakened by what happened. They feel that they don't have the same level of social power, control and reputation that they did prior to the offense. They feel they have to retaliate in order to be restored. Forgive is the last thing they want to do.

In truth, their sense of power and influence were probably tenuous in the first place. Otherwise there would not have been the need to prove themselves by hurting someone else, even when they have been hurt. They have difficulty seeing the innocence of the one who hurt them. And the need to strike out may be overwhelming. Unfortunately, if they do retaliate, as I mentioned earlier, the relief, unbeknownst to them, may be very short lived.

In order to get to the place of forgiveness, this person has to have a source of validation that is internal rather than external. They have to recover their sense of self from within. They may benefit from counseling to help them establish a sense of self-worth that is not based on the opinions of others.

Another barrier to forgiveness is the need to protect oneself. It often happens that the one who hurt you is someone close. That means that there was a sense of trust that was betrayed. They weren't supposed to do what they did. They weren't supposed to abuse, abandon, neglect or reject you the way they did. They broke your trust. The fear is that now you've become vulnerable to being hurt more. The unanswered question is whether or not forgiving will open the doors wide for them to be more aggressive towards you. There really isn't any way to tell immediately.

Passing time provides information that isn't readily available initially. Things like change in the behavior and attitude of the offender cannot be known except with time. If the abuse was repeated, will that change now? How will forgiving them make a difference? Even the sincerest desire to forgive can be sidelined by the lack of remorse or of an authentic apology from the offender. The one who refuses to forgive under these circumstances may be attempting to regain some sense of equal footing in the relationship. To reach a place of forgiveness, the one hurt must know it is their right to set boundaries and how to do that effectively. Only when they have a real sense that they are safe from future attack, that the offender is sincerely remorseful, and that the apology is authentic, can they entertain the possibility of forgiving.

Remember, forgiveness is a decision. It takes a purposeful, intentional choice to forgive. It may be a process and not something that happens in an instant. Forgiveness may take practice over time. It may not be easy to overcome these barriers. It helps to understand the barriers that may be in the way of your forgiveness. Acknowledge them. Then do what you must to get past them.

What is Forgiveness?

So, what is forgiveness anyway? It's time for a working definition. Generally speaking, the psychological community defines forgiveness as *an intentional, chosen decision to let go of resentful, vengeful feelings toward a person or persons who have hurt you or caused you harm, regardless of whether they deserve to be forgiven.* Generally, I believe forgiving should have nothing to do with the offender. Remember forgiving is about your well-being, your health, your peace.

It might be helpful at this juncture to talk a bit about what forgiveness **isn't**.

- *Forgiveness doesn't mean forgetting.*

  People always say, "I can forgive, but I'll never forget." Authentic forgiveness does not require forgetting the offense. It does require letting the other off the hook for the offense. It does include not holding the offense against the other after it has been forgiven.

- *Forgiveness doesn't mean reconciliation.*

  As in forgiveness with married couples, forgiveness may mean we still divorce. I can forgive you and still not want to continue in the relationship, regardless of the circumstances.

- *Forgiveness doesn't mean acceptance.*

  In many cases the violation occurred on such a deep level that to accept it means to violate one's own sense of self. To place oneself in a "lesser than" position during forgiveness means to neglect your own personhood in favor of the offender. That is not forgiveness. Forgiveness does not condone the offense or minimize the impact of it.

- *Forgiveness doesn't mean I'm over it completely all at once.*

  Forgiveness is a process. It is possible to bounce back and forth between forgiving and hurting back to forgiving and back to hurting for some time. Eventually, with decisiveness and courage, the hurt lessens, and the forgiveness grows. Give it the healing time it deserves.

- *Forgiveness doesn't mean that I like you again.*

  Forgiveness does not necessarily mean that I have warm, fuzzy feelings toward you again. It could mean that I decide to keep my distance until, if, trust is re-built. Forgiveness empowers the offended to acknowledge the pain without allowing the pain to define them.

How-to-Forgive Process

Here is the process I used to forgive everyone who hurt me in my life. I'll share the overarching themes, then I'll share the nitty gritty work that it takes to forgive.

1. *Know who you are.*

   It is vastly important that you are familiar with yourself. You need to know what makes you happy, mad, sad, frustrated, upset, uncomfortable, etc. Get in touch with your emotions and what makes you tick. This knowledge helps you form a baseline of inner strength that you will need to overcome the hurt you've suffered.

2. *Know that it's all right to forgive yourself.*

   a. Don't be so hard on yourself. No matter what you did, own it.

   b. We go through a process of learning and in that process, we will make some decisions we're not all right with or regret later. We have to know that as we know better, we do better. It doesn't matter if you've done the same thing repeatedly. When you get it and want to do better, then you will. Trust yourself and your instincts.

3. *Forgive others.*

   a. Know that it's all right to let a person go.

   b. Try not to get even.

   c. Why should we allow others to control our temperament? Why should we allow others to get and keep us mentally, emotionally, physically bound? We are responsible and in charge of our own peace of mind. It's not helping you, carrying all that weight. Stress kills slowly. Don't allow that to be your story. Let them go.

4. *Love on you.*

    a. Take the time to spend time with you. Get to loving on you.

    b. Set boundaries and know what you will and won't tolerate or accept. You have control over what you allow in your personal space.

    c. Rid yourself of negativity.

    d. Hold on to you. Hug you. Do what you love to do and enjoy. Treat yourself for freeing yourself.

5. *Soaring! Moving into the new You!*

Now it's time to turn the page to a new you. You're lighter, you're at peace; don't look back. Move forward into your greatness!

Before you begin this process, please prepare yourself to be challenged. It is very important that you take time as you go through this and take good care of yourself. If you have a support person, it might be a good idea to let them know you will be starting this process and have them on standby should things get a little tough to handle on your own. I say this because there can be some deep emotions that could surface through this process. You just want to be sure you are safe and well cared for as you do this. If having support in this way is a challenge for you, as in, you have difficulty asking for help, make a decision now that you will not go any further without having someone stand for your healing and wholeness. Make the call, have the conversation, ask for help. Do it now.

Follow the steps in order at first. There is a logical sequence to them. Then if you need to revisit one of them for a deeper dive, do that once you have completed the sequence at least once. I encourage you to get a notebook just for this process. There is a lot that can come up that you may not have even known was related to unforgiveness before you did this. Having a dedicated notebook helps to keep the process pure and easy.

Ready?

Here we go…

To begin, sit quietly in a space where you will not be disturbed. If you need to hang a "Do Not Disturb" sign on the door and turn off the phone, do that. You should consider this a sacred time that you've set aside for yourself. You deserve this time to yourself.

Take out a clean sheet of paper and a favorite writing instrument.

1. *Acknowledge that everyone who has hurt you does not need to be forgiven.* It's important to make that distinction. It can be overwhelming to ruminate on how much we have been hurt or taken advantage of. The list you are making here is only comprised of those whose offense has hurt you significantly enough that forgiveness is in order. Start by identifying a hurt that is current for you. Write the person's name and the offense. Using a Subjective Units of Distress Scale or SUDS, ask yourself on a scale of 1 (enough pain to need forgiveness) to 10 (worst pain imaginable), how deep is the hurt you feel about this issue? Place the score next to the offense. Continue listing all the current hurts you can with the person's name, the offense and the SUDS score.

2. *Decide which you want to address first.*

3. *Consider the hurt you have before you.* Read it out loud. Close your eyes, take a deep breath and notice where in your body you feel the hurt. Write it down.

4. *Hear the words that were said about or to you by this person.* Where do they land for you? What is the thought that comes with hearing those words? Write them down.

5. *Consider now, how has your life been affected by this person's offense?* What are the negative impacts? What are the positive impacts (e.g. lessons learned)? Consider any psychological, emotional, mental or physical harm there may have been. Write them down.

6. *Think now about how your world views have changed, if at all.* Have you changed your views on anyone outside of this situation? Maybe globalized your thoughts? An example may be, "I'll never trust men again." Or "I don't want anything to do with anybody's church ever!" Write it down.

7. *Acknowledge and recognize for yourself, what happened was not acceptable.* Allow yourself to feel whatever comes to the surface, good, bad or ugly.

8. *Look at what you've written down.* Take another deep breath and check in. Is there anything left to acknowledge? Is there something left that needs to be added to the list? Add it now.

9. *Take another deep breath.* When you feel ready to do so, make the decision to forgive. Say this out loud: "(Name of Person), I forgive you." If that is still too big a leap, say the following out loud: "Maybe I want to forgive (Name of Person). Maybe I am willing to forgive (Name of Person). Part of me feels able to forgive (Name of Person). And that's enough right now."

10. *The decision to forgive includes the decision to let go of the offense.* It also includes your decision about what forgiveness looks like. Will you continue the relationship as it is? Will you put new boundaries in place? Will you have a conversation with the offender about the offense and your forgiveness? How will your forgiveness be

shown? Will you begin to act differently toward this person? Will you demonstrate more kindness, generosity, consideration? Forgiveness may or may not include deliberately attempting to reduce resentment, anger, avoidance, etc. toward this person. Decide what it means for you.

11. *Go back to the original list and use the same process for each offender.*

Sometimes the difference between forgiving and not forgiving is being able to see the offender's innocence. Of course, this is a lot more challenging when the offense was intentional. Still, it is possible to see the other's innocence. It may just take a little more digging and a brighter light to shine on the situation.

Seeing the offender's innocence means being willing to give them the benefit of the doubt. The "Benefit of the Doubt" means to think something positive about someone instead of something negative when you could legitimately choose either one. It means that you willingly decide to believe they meant no harm. The benefit of the doubt looks beyond the behavior, the insult, the harm, the offense to attempt to see that the offense was unintentional or could not be avoided. There is a certain level of natural forgiveness in giving the benefit of the doubt.

Consider this: if a blind man stepped on your foot, would you be offended? Probably not. You would look beyond the event or behavior and give him much grace and consideration. You might even be the one apologizing for having your foot in his way! However, if after stepping on your foot, you saw him take his glasses off, fold up his cane and walk with perfect sight down the hall, that's a whole different matter. Now you have an offense, and how dare he!

The same holds true for those who offend us who have mental/emotional issues, addictions and other issues that we cannot see. Just because we can't see them does not mean they are not there and impacting the relationship. Whether you agree with it or not, the fact remains that these kinds of issues affect the way the sufferer thinks. It therefore affects too the way they conduct themselves in relationships.

Now of course the argument could be made that, barring some congenital birth defect, there were decisions made to create the present circumstance. And because of that, there are no excuses that can be made for the offensive behavior. Substance users and other addicts chose to use. Addicts, regardless of the addiction, have rocky relationships. The substance thinking takes over.

How could I have held anything against my mom? As an addict, she was doing the best she could with the physical, mental, emotional, and spiritual resources she had. She also had the need for self-preservation. Many times, her very life was threatened. Although the physical, neurological changes in brain functioning from prolonged substance use are proven, addicts nonetheless chose to use. What we overlook too often, I believe, is that behind the substance use is often basic human emotions. Fear and the need for safety are high on the list. What could I in good conscience have held against my mother? She was just as scared as I was. She needed just as much protection as I did. Age didn't matter. Look at what she endured. She got high to deal with the circumstances of her life. The violence threatened her life daily. Sometimes we have to look beyond the offense to see the frightened person beneath it.

Here's Your Next Forgiveness Challenge:

Ask yourself the following questions about the offender, the person who hurt you:

- What is life like for this person?

- What was life like while they were growing up?

- What physical, emotional or mental health wounds did they experience growing up that could have made them more likely to hurt you?

- What kinds of pressure or stress was this person going through at the time they offended you?

Asking these questions serves to help understand the other person's perspective, much as we expect, or would like, them to understand and consider ours. *They in no way excuse or condone the other person's behavior.* They simply identify possible reasons behind the behavior. They rather serve to better understand the other person's vulnerability and humanness...same as ours.

That brings us to the next step in forgiveness. You must come into greater awareness of the offender's humanness. Can you begin, on any level, to see them as a hurting, vulnerable human? Even if there was intentionality behind the offense, it does not remove their humanness.

In very general terms, it can be said that there are basic human needs. In the traditional needs expressed on Maslow's Hierarchy of Needs, biological needs and safety and security needs are the first two.

1. *Biological and physiological needs* – air, food, drink, shelter, warmth, sex, sleep.

2. *Safety needs* – protection from elements, security, order, law, stability, freedom from fear.

3. *Love and belongingness needs* – friendship, intimacy, trust, acceptance, receiving and giving affection and love. Affiliating, being part of a group (family, friends, work).

4. *Esteem needs* – which Maslow classified into two categories: (i) esteem for oneself (dignity, achievement, mastery, independence) and (ii) the desire for reputation or respect from others (e.g., status, prestige). Maslow indicated that the need for respect or reputation is most important for children and adolescents and precedes real self-esteem or dignity.

5. *Self-actualization needs* – realizing personal potential, self-fulfillment, seeking personal growth

and peak experiences. A desire "to become everything one is capable of becoming."

Maslow, A. H. (1987). *Motivation and personality (3rd ed.)*. Delhi, India: Pearson Education. p. 64.

Neither my mom nor anyone else in my immediate family had these basic needs met...not even remotely. The ongoing violence reduced the sense of safety to nothing in our lives. There was often no food. When you look at the story behind the story, it looks to me like Mom did everything she could, everything she was able to do for me. I don't believe she thought I would be abused in the house where she left me. She was trying to keep me safe and get me away from the violence at home. She did what she thought was best for me. Should I have expected her to check out the home first? She couldn't be in control of who visited or stayed. Like I thought when my dad wanted me to move to Oklahoma to live with her, how could she help me take care of my baby when she couldn't take care of me...or herself?

Your task in this part of your forgiveness journey is to humanize the offender to the best of your ability. Pay attention to any little spark of compassion you may have towards them. Can you see that they may have been confused, frightened, overwhelmed, grieving, stressed, misinformed, misguided, mistaken or something else? Is it possible they regret their actions?

Another human frailty is to displace emotions. A displaced emotion is one that is redirected from the original source to another one that feels safer. It is not appropriate, nor is it acceptable. It is simply a choice for safety. Displacing emotions happens frequently and unconsciously. Displaced emotions can be the source of offense. Being an unconsciously expressed emotion means it is probably an issue of anger, disappointment, rejection, abuse, neglect or some other negative experience.

Consciously becoming aware of your own and the offender's pain helps you not throw your pain off on someone else. You may be just as guilty of displacing your emotions as your offender. Maturely handling your own pain will keep you from perpetrating your own offense on some unsuspecting innocent family member or friend, or even back on the one who offended you.

There is a saying: "Hurting people hurt people." That's just the way it is, unfortunately. Everyone is not emotionally mature enough to handle their emotions appropriately. When we have been emotionally wounded and are emotionally immature, our tendency is to displace our pain onto others. Unless this is managed, it could be the start or continuation of a painful legacy of anger, rejection, abuse, neglect and disappointment.

A technique that can help the process of forgiveness is to consider a gift of some kind that you can give to the person you are trying to forgive. Now, I know this may make you raise your eyebrow a bit. *Shouldn't the offender be coming to you with a peace offering? What sense does it make for you to give a gift to the one who hurt you?* Well, think of it this way: Forgiveness is the act of extending the olive branch. It, in itself, is an act of peace. For you to offer a gift to the one who hurt you is like you showing mercy where there may have been none for you. The gift you offer may be no more than a phone call, a card, or even just a smile. It only has to be a showing of mercy. Certainly, you have to consider your own safety when extending the olive branch. Never place yourself in danger. If there is no way to safely extend the kindness or consideration, then by all means, be okay with doing nothing of direct kindness toward that person. Maybe you then simply send them well wishes from afar.

A worthwhile exercise is to find meaning in your experience. For instance, those who find themselves repeatedly in the midst of chaos and confusion or within a thematic framework of similar experiences, may do well to explore what they may be doing to create the chaos. There may also be an opportunity to become more sensitive to the needs of others as they attempt to understand their own pain.

There is another aspect of forgiveness that needs to be addressed here. It is the concept of "Letting go." Humans are creatures of habit. Just like it says in Maslow's Hierarchy, the basic needs are the same for all of us. How those needs get expressed and subsequently met may be completely different for each of us. That is what makes "letting go" a challenge. They say that water seeks the lowest level. So do we, in some regard. What I mean by that is many times, humans look to keep status quo, even in the case of a violent, abusive past. Generally speaking, we tend to choose the known over the unknown. We already know how to do what we do. There are all kinds of ways that we mentally trick ourselves into staying stuck.

As humans we tend to be risk-avoidant. Because of the need for safety and security, we understandably seek the known and predictable. The difficult part comes when the known and predictable is chaos and confusion, drama and danger.

Children like I was, who grew up to know nothing other than rejection and abandonment, tend to recreate that same pattern unconsciously. It's not intentional; it is just what we know. Interestingly, it is what we are comfortable with.

Our motivation comes through having what we want some of the time. It's called *intermittent reinforcement and motivation*. Our expectation is not to have what we want most of the time. In our lives we have come to understand that that is not likely to happen. That's especially significant if you grew up starved for love, acceptance, approval, and support. Even the slightest hint of any of that was a feast.

We also tend to see life through rose-colored glasses. Anything can be interpreted as positive. A complete and total loss becomes a "near win." For me, it was being free to do whatever I wanted, whenever I wanted. Never mind that there was no parental supervision. That just left me more time to drink, smoke and whatever. It worked for me. It's like people playing slot machines. Two of a kind that match is a near win, not a loss. *Next time it'll be better. Next time I'll win.* For me, it was "Dad will take me with him for a fresh start this time." "Mom will come back for me this time." There was always hope for the next promise. Any little sliver of something to hold on to was enough to hang my dreams on.

Living that way brought me to a place where I had to learn to let go. I had to learn to let go of the past and everything it held and taught me. I had to learn to let go of expectations, reasonable ones and unreasonable. I had to learn to stop ruminating on the pain and let it go. If my desire was to create a new future, I had to let go of my past. I would be a prisoner of past hurts and disappointments until I did.

What Letting Go Isn't

It is important to know what "letting go" means. It does not mean that the past didn't happen. It doesn't mean that I can pretend that what happened to me didn't happen to me. It doesn't mean that I wasn't hurt, abandoned, abused, molested, neglected and all of the rest. It doesn't mean that I let my parents off the hook completely for how their decisions impacted my life. My dads are still accountable for their decisions and how I was affected by them. The distinction is that I have learned what I can trust them for and what I can't. That is a really important lesson to learn.

Letting go means learning to discern between the healthy ways of thinking and toxic thoughts. You must grow to maturity in your thoughts and perspectives, being willing to let go of feelings that keep you stuck. It becomes essential to adopt ways of thinking and understanding that move you forward. Letting go means to stop being stopped. I didn't know it then, but I was engaged in a process called Goal Disengagement.

Goal Disengagement is a four-step process. It guides the user through a system for letting go of the thinking processes that continue the status quo (*cognitive disengagement*). It manages the emotions that go along with giving up (*affective disengagement*). It gives up the earlier goal (*motivational disengagement*). And it creates action plans for a new goal (*behavioral disengagement*). Each step in the disengagement process requires a slightly different set of skills.

Through cognitive disengagement, you stop ruminating about the past and suffered losses. You stop thinking about losses and why you didn't achieve your goals. You stop the "what ifs" that would have you hold on to the goal you need to relinquish. With affective disengagement, you address any emotions that are stimulated when you fail. Typically, these include guilt, low self-esteem, low self-worth, grief, loss of hope, etc. Through motivational disengagement, you let go of the current goal and put a new one in place, complete with new objectives. And finally, behavioral disengagement requires you to begin to behave in new ways to act on changing your future.

How I Recovered from a Toxic Childhood and Learned to Forgive

What I discovered is that in my childhood, I did what I needed to do to survive. I felt unloved, unseen, and marginalized. I was subjected to endless criticism, abuse and neglect. I did what I needed to armor and protect myself and eventually my children. I did what I could in my teens to be safe and have what I needed. I moved around until I had the support I needed to make life work.

All the while I was making decisions about what I wanted in life and what I didn't want in life. I started making my own choices when I had to make them, even before I became a teen. I was also making decisions about how to deal with my family in a way that made sense for me. Mine was not a traditional family by any means. Just consider the fact that I didn't even know my own name until my teens.

I relished my freedom, though I longed for something I could rely upon. When I realized my family was not reliable and I had to let go of the hope that they ever would be was when I started to grow up and mature. It's when my efforts to manage life "normally" began to fail – I was still hurt by run-ins with my parents and challenged in managing my emotions. I still felt lost and unable to set healthy boundaries. I felt stuck. I had to find a new way to understand and relate to my family. I had to learn to let go. I had to learn to disengage.

Cognitive disengagement is more difficult and challenging. There are so many cultural expectations about family, mother and father. There are expectations about how to relate to mother and how to relate to father. We are supposed to relate to mother and father with respect, even though they may not be respectable. Those titles hold a lot of meaning in our culture.

Affective disengagement is the most difficult of all aspects of disengagement. Letting go of the feelings is hard. It's hard to get your feet under you to know what is real and what is not. The past pain seems connected to every other feeling, and your emotions make you question yourself and your choices. Then, there is the fear that what they say about you is true and you're just not worthy of love.

My core conflict is demonstrated through motivational disengagement. As a daughter, I wanted more than anything for my mother to love and accept me. When that didn't happen, I was essentially forced to find a new way of relating to my mother, while still wanting her approval. This dichotomy kept me living the status quo until I could break out of it. And as long as the core conflict continues, changing the expectation of family is nearly impossible.

Letting Go in Small Steps

These are the steps that helped me let go of the status quo and create a new life for myself and my children:

- Recognize it's not your fault.
- Stop blaming yourself. Let yourself off the hook. Stop looking for what you could have done differently or done better. Accept that your parents made some choices that had a distinct impact on your life that you had to manage, not change.
- Don't normalize abusive behavior.
- Regardless of how much you were exposed to, recognize that abuse is not normal. It does not have to be reconstructed in your life. You can choose differently. You can choose to be healthy and happy. Recognize abuse for what it is: Emotional Sickness.

- Set healthy boundaries and rules for how you will be treated and regarded, and *stick to them*, calmly and consistently.

- Learn what is "me-not-me," "mine-not-mine." Every relationship has boundaries. You are the keeper of yours. Learn to manage your relationship respectful of your boundaries and everyone else's.

- Build your emotional skill set. Learn to identify your emotions. Know what you feel when you feel it. Be precise in your definition of your feelings. Develop your emotional IQ. Be able to trace the source of your feelings, whatever they are, especially when they are negative or troubling.

- Manage your thoughts. Learn to control or stop your thoughts. Stop ruminating and rehearsing negative thoughts. Thoughts evoke feelings that match them. Therefore, negative thoughts equal negative feelings. You can manage the thoughts that source the feelings. Worried rumination will keep you completely stuck.

What to Do When You Can't Forgive

As a forgiveness coach, my job is to help people learn to forgive. But are there times when forgiveness is not the answer? I believe forgiveness is always the way to go. I say this not because of my own journey, but because I don't think there is ever a situation or circumstance where you stand to gain nothing by forgiving. However, I do believe there is a great deal to lose by not forgiving. If, as I have postulated through this work, forgiveness is all about you and what you stand to gain by forgiving, then how can you go wrong? You stand to reap all the benefits.

Sometimes acceptance is the key. With acceptance can come closure. Acceptance is believing that a person or situation doesn't have to be any different than it is. This is still not condoning a behavior or situation, but it is acknowledging that it happened and agreeing with yourself that it no longer has control over your life. Forgiveness can still occur within the boundaries of acceptance.

Traditional forgiveness says the key is healthy boundaries, healthy regard for one another, respect, etc. The challenge comes in when we are exposed to someone who repeatedly harms us, who doesn't take responsibility for themselves and to whom we give many, many, many opportunities to start over. That is moving into the realm of enabling – not a healthy relationship by any means. In that situation, while forgiving is vital, not forgetting is also important so that you don't allow the situation to repeat.

I want to reiterate that forgiveness is a process, and not one that needs to be rushed. It is acceptable to give yourself permission to not forgive in the moment. Allow yourself the opportunity to process the way you need to, for as long as you need to. This book was not written to force forgiveness on you. It is meant to share the benefits of forgiveness and the process of how to forgive. I acknowledge you for wanting to forgive and for exploring forgiveness.

The Bottom Line

It really is okay not to forgive someone if you're not ready to. That's your choice; you can forgive or not. Having said that, it's also important to explore why you're not ready to forgive. Are there underlying issues that need to be addressed to support your preparation to forgive? Are there underlying thoughts, feelings, and experiences that are more all-encompassing?

I've learned to be gentle with myself where my feelings and forgiveness are concerned. I know how to forgive, and I know when I'm ready to forgive. Give the same gift to yourself. I'm not bitter, angry, or stuck in my personal growth because of how I've chosen to support myself through the process of forgiving myself. In that process, I've stopped believing things should be any different than they are. I accept and celebrate my own feelings and experiences, and I accept everyone else involved for who they are and how they show up too. I've created healthy, necessary boundaries, and healthy relationships, especially with my children. And I've grown in ways I could only imagine when I was a child. I'm a stronger person for that.

Wesley

Because I forgave my biological father, Wesley, I was able to have a conversation with him about my mom and his relationship with her. It was eye-opening and unexpectedly tender to hear. I am certain that this conversation would not have been possible had I not done the work of forgiving him. Because he and my mother were never together during my lifetime, I did not have the background story about their connection and romance. You will recall that I was raised to believe that Wesley was my godfather until I was in my teens. By then I had already been dropped off at a stranger's home, where I spent several years sleeping on the couch or on the floor, and where I had been molested. During this time, Wesley was still in the picture, though my mom was with someone else. I appreciate my dad's sharing this story with me. It gave me a context and understanding for what was happening to me and why. Our relationship is four years old now. We are being knitted together as family. The road is still rocky, but there is a greater desire for connection now than ever. Here is the transcript of that conversation:

Wesley: I'd get off work early, about maybe 4:30, quarter to 5...There was a little parking lot right alongside the apartment, efficiency in the back like with the stairs that go up and down, and then my apartment was, I had a regular one-bedroom apartment and I think she had the balcony at that time on the back end, and she could just come out her door and come right down the steps. She was on the third floor, come right down the steps, and she'd hang clothes out there. Had one of those laundry pulls, get the clothes, and hang them up.

So, I came from work, backed in, I usually backed in to the lot. I never parked on the street. So, I parked the car and everything and happened to just look up, so she waved, and I waved, "Hey." Okay. So, she, as I was coming up the steps, she was just standing up there, she was still hanging clothes and I told her my name and everything, so I asked her how long she'd been there, and she said she'd been there for a while. I said, "Well dag, all this time I never noticed you being here." and she said, "Well I never really come out except for hanging up clothes this way, the back way." I said, "Well that makes sense." So, I just went on, I guess we sat there and talked for a little while. She said, "I always see you. I see you coming in," and stuff. "Around this time, I'll be looking out the window." And I was like, "Whaaat?" She said, "Yeah," so I said, "Okay."

So I went on back in the house, back to my place and did my thing, fixed my dinner and everything, and that was it. And then, the day was over. And I was thinking, I couldn't believe she was there all that time, and for one thing, boy I'll tell you, she had the prettiest smile I ever seen in my life. That's the thing, that's what really, really got me, that smile of hers. And then I kept, I couldn't stop thinking half the night, "What in the world? How could I not see that? What's going on?" Of course, working so much, that's all I've ever done, work, come home, do your thing.

So, I did the same ole thing again, went home, went on to work the next morning, and same ole thing, so next day I came by, I drove back in the lot there, she was sitting on the second floor. And on the step, they were like orange steps back there, and she was sitting there, and so we started talking again, there goes that smile again, we just started talking again, so that's the way, I was asking her about her place and all, she was telling me she had a little baby named Clay. That's when Clay was real little; he was in his crib asleep at the time. She had the door open up there and said, "I got the door open, so I can hear him." I said, "Okay." So we just talked in general, different things, so I told her about my situation, I was separated and stuff at the time, and I'd been up there for a while. I was telling Mom – my mom lived up in the front part of the building, in the high rise, she lived up on the second floor, on the next floor, I lived up on the second floor back. So, I was back there by the water, where the efficiencies were, and she was out front, where you can look at the freeway out there. And so, we sat there and talked until just about, I guess, it was getting dark, we were just standing out there, just talking, went in the house a couple times to see what Clay was doing, and we'd come back out, and she said, "I've gotta get on in," and I said, "Well, me too, I gotta get home and get me something to eat, I'm kinda hungry," and I went back in there, got me something to eat, and it just kept going like that, it was like that the next day and the next day, it was basically the same stuff. And then I still didn't really – I didn't think it was too much of anything at that time, then finally, I would ask her what was she doing or whatever and asked her to come over and have something to eat or something like that.

She said, "I'd like that." And I said, "All right that's good." So, that was the first time I ever had a woman in my house since the separation. So that's what she done, she came over and we ate, I forgot what we ate, but we sat there and ate and then go back, so we'd just do that, we'd do our thing, listening to music, mostly sit there, it was one of those things, like a semi-relationship. And she went on back to her place and I went to my place. That's how it went. So, then after – I'd give it a good month, two months, I'd say about two months, and then, over the weekend time, it had rained hard. It rained, I mean it was rainy, and so she, by her being up on the third floor, she said, oh I know, she came to my apartment, banging on the door, and said the ceiling fell, and fell into Clay's crib. She said she had just got Clay out of there. She had taken him to the kitchen because she was heating up milk for him. And she went in the kitchen, and she said she heard this big noise, and she didn't know what to do, go out the front door or go back in there where the noise was coming from, which was the bedroom. And she decided she'd peep, so she went on back in there and looked. And there wasn't a light on because the ceiling that fell had the light and everything, come down in one part. So, she went on and saw that the ceiling had fell in to Clay's crib. So, when she come downstairs, of course, and banged on my door, she had Clay in her hands at the time, so I said, "Well, I'll take a look at it." So, I didn't realize it was as bad as it was! Man, it was messed up! I mean that whole part of the ceiling just fell. And not only that, a rat was in there, an old dried-up rat, or I guess a rat grew up in there in the attic, and when it fell, it was all in his crib. So, I went up there. I got my flashlight, that's how come I saw everything, I got my flashlight. And sure enough man, it would have been really a terrible situation if she hadn't gotten him out of the crib like that. It was just 10-15 minutes, just enough time for her to pick him up, go in the kitchen and heat the milk up, it was within that time! I told her, "Look, you cannot stay in here." She had made a couple calls, she asked me could she use the phone to make a call. I said, "Look, you all, you stay with me, come down, stay in my apartment." She said, "Are you sure?" I said, "Yeah," I said, "You can't stay up there like that, plus you don't know, you gotta get in touch with the landlord and let him know what's going on, for one thing. You can't take that baby back up there like that." And then she was trying to clean the crib out, and I said, "Forget about that, we'll deal with that later." So that's what she done, she come on down, and Clay stayed on the couch for a while, and she brought his pampers and all like that, had to bring them down, so that's really how everything started, basically, by that rat being up there. (laughs)

That story's the start of the relationship. Like I said, it was just one of them things, she even told my mom, I went to work, I just kept seeing her face, that smile, ahh man, I couldn't get over that smile, I kept seeing that face and I'd be working, and I'd say, "Oh man," she had a smile and a half on her. I could just see it, when I first saw her, when she was standing up there hanging up the clothes is what really done it. She just had that smile, it was just a new kind of thing, and it's actually the way the relationship started, from the incident, basically.

I think this was near a weekend, had to be, because either a Saturday night or a Sunday, yeah, a Sunday, because she couldn't get in touch with the landlord until Monday. That's what it was. Of course, I had to go to work, so she stayed there at the house. And when I got back, I asked her had she got in touch with anybody, so she said, "Yeah, they came over here and looked and everything and the guy just came over here and shook his head because there's nothing they could do about it. She could get it fixed or whatever she wants because she was staying somewhere else at the time, but I told her "Don't even think about going back up in there. Stay here." So that's how it all really started right there.

It went on, and went on, for all that time, and then that's when Olivia and Leah came back, and that was a really messed up part. Well, hey, I just had to tell her straight up, what was going on. I told her I can't, I'm NOT going to put her out, I'm going to keep her here and Clay, so you'll have to deal with it, that's all I know. That was going on, she had the, the car was all packed up with the clothes and everything, oh that was terrible. Oh, that was it, that's a messed-up day right there. Or night, evening, it was like 9:00 at night, or so, 8:30-9:00. Car was filled with everything and I had to go down there and tell her the situation. Only thing she could say was "Okay." (laughs) Start the car, back up, and there they go, back off, that was it. That was the end of another relationship basically. She felt bad about the situation and I said, "Well, hey, wasn't nothing you could do." I wouldn't let you stay up there like that when you don't know what else is gonna happen. Don't even worry about it. I made my decision, and that's the way it was.

I was paying all the bills there at the house, and wasn't really nothing said, she wouldn't say it to me directly, it might have been indirectly. Because I mean, what could you say? She waited too long, in other words, so, I felt bad about it for a few minutes, then I said well it's not that she don't have anywhere to go, because she can go back to her parents anyway. That's how that went.

Everything was really, really good, it turned out pretty good.

Yvonne: How long did y'all stay there?

Wesley: At the apartment? We stayed at the apartment, I guess a good, all that year, when the lease was up, we were looking for more like a bigger place. We looked at a place that was on Van Buren Street, and that's where we went from there, Van Buren Street. It was nice, they had just redone the apartment and everything, it had two bedrooms, bath, living room, had a little dining room area, and had a little porch. And other people, the second floor, they went around the side and went up that way, but they didn't have a porch or anything, they had a little balcony, but it was like right out from their window, so it wasn't really like the porch we had. It was beautiful. We stayed there for a year, stayed at Van Buren for a whole year, then after that, we went to live with my pop. That's when he was buying and selling houses, so we went there.

I went there to look at the place he bought. He just bought a place and threw me the keys and said, "Here, go in there and see what has to be done." (laughs) He had to get the electric turned on and I go in there to check it out and found what was all going on, and of course I do the painting and everything. I do the painting, he got people to do the other quality work that needed to be done, to get it all fixed up to rent out. That's what he done. It was a whole house, five bedrooms! Five bedrooms, two baths, big living room, big dining room, kitchen, pantry out in back of the kitchen, then you go out to the backyard, there was a backyard. So, we stayed there for close to two years, because after I got it finished I decided I wanted it for myself. (laughs) So that's what I done. I said, "Look, I think I like this house, I think I wanna take it." And then he said, "Well, it's up to you, I got another one lined up too, so work on that one." I had the option to keep whatever I wanted at the time, and it wasn't no big deal, he'd just get another house and do the same thing. And of course, I still had my job, I'd go to my job, then after I got off work I'd do all that other stuff. So, I got it in living condition, basically, enough to move in. Like I say, he got the electric and everything on. So then, he didn't have to sign another lease for the next year, we didn't have to sign no lease or nothing. We got out of there a month ahead of time. And went on over there to 6th Street to stay. And this was, I will say, around Van Buren Street, around 7th and Ambrose, the pub bar was on 6th and Cleveland, it was not that far from it. We didn't have nothing to do but just move from one place to the other. And that was it. Clay came along, of course, with us too. He was walking and everything then. (laughs) He had his hat on and a little room back there, the main thing was trying to keep him in it because every time we'd leave, boy he'd be hollering and carrying on. Had to go up and get him and bring him downstairs for a while until he actually fell asleep. It was really nice.

Yvonne: How'd I come along?

Wesley: Very complicated. (laughs) When you came along, you came along without me knowing you came along, actually. So that was…when you came along…

Yvonne: *You was saying something about you was at work and somebody came over the house or Pop said something about somebody coming over.*

Wesley: Yeah, he did, when I came home he was telling me, because he would usually stop by at will, at random, never know when he was coming by, of course that was his house or whatever, so he, a lot of times, he'd go on in there and get coffee and stuff like that. I always kept a coffee pot in there just in case he came around. He's the one that got me started drinking coffee, actually. So, he bought me my first coffee pot. So, he said, "When I come around I want this coffee on, I always want me a cup of coffee when I'm here," so I said, "Okay." He got one that done everything by itself, automatically, it started up in the morning, then it stays around, and I went to work, but he'd come all through the day, like I say, and so then he asked me did I know, trying to remember what he was telling me, in a roundabout way, he was telling me that there was somebody there at the house every time he went over there. And said, did I know who he was. I said, "No," I said she always told me a cousin was there, and stuff like that, so he'd look at me and say, "Okay" (laughs). He'd say, with that curious mind he had, he'd never really come out and say too much of anything, he'd just look at me like, "Oookayyy…If that's the way you want to think…" Of course, I didn't think that way. I just thought the way it was. So that's how that went. I thought it was a cousin that he'd seen around. There was another girl too that would come around there. I forgot her name.

Yvonne: Sherry.

Wesley: Oh, you know about Sherry? Yeah, Sherry. That was your mom's best girlfriend. And then she would come over there at times and they'd sit there. Then she'd go on about her business, go home. So that's the way that went. After that, I guess a good couple three months went by, as far as I was concerned it was okay. I went along, and I asked her what was going on, so she would say that was her cousin too, so there I go…I didn't think too much about it. So finally, it just got to a point that I thought, this don't sound right here, I figured out what's going on…Well I told her the best thing to do is just go ahead and leave. That was the best thing because it was just getting outrageous. Because I mean, more than likely, he didn't really respect the house, or nothing like that. We never really got into it, because I didn't think it would, he had anything to do with it, it was more like me and her, me and your mom basically. We had a couple arguments about it, and I just couldn't believe it, I had gone out and hearing the different things I heard and stuff like that, so I said "Well, I think the best thing for you to do is just leave." So that's basically what she done. Packed her clothes and just went. That was the end of that. Of course, like I say, little light arguments here and there. He didn't really have that much to say to me. Not really. I never really got into it with him, because most of the time whenever that incident was happening, was in the car basically, they'd pull up or something like that, go out and sit in the car for hours and smoked herb or however that went. That's what it was all about then mostly, and I just went in the house and got my dinner like normal, and wait till she come on in. And then after we got in an argument a couple of times, the situation was odd, and I think there was more to it than what she was telling me. So, she was always saying, "You believe Pop over me, which one you believe, your Pop or me?" Or however it went. I said, "Well Pop is around here the majority of the time, so I don't think he would steer me in the wrong direction." So that's how that went.

Yvonne: And then, how did I come about, like how did you find out about me?

Wesley: I didn't until you, until, well she had called, and told me they lived on Miller Road or something like that.

Yvonne: So, the whole time after she left, y'all didn't talk anymore?

Wesley: Not really. Not really because there wasn't that much to talk about after that. It's just one of them things, we didn't say anything for the next two or three months. Really nothing because the next time, I think we had talked one or two times after that or something like that. And so, I don't, I don't, I really can't figure out how that went. My main thing, I was working and that sort of kept my mind occupied most of the time. It was just her choice how, whatever, however she wanted to do. And of course, the conversation had come up about marrying, before, I would say I didn't want to get married at that time. But she didn't give me, of course, no reason, no reason at all. And so, things just went the way they went.

After that, I ran into her brother, I think it was, Ivan, remember him? I would run into him all the time. We'd get to talking. He just told me that they were getting ornery and he'd be beating on her. I said, "Beating on her? Beating on her for what?" He asked me had I heard from your mom, Yvonne, I said, "No, I hadn't heard from her in at least a couple weeks," or whatever, "and she never mentioned anything like that!"

So, I guess this was happening all along, it was just messed-up weekends for her, basically. Then after that is when the hospital thing came. And of course, that was, I guess, more than likely, had to be posted like three or four months, or I'd say two, because she wasn't going anymore, she left the house. That's when I ran into Ivan. That's the only person I was gonna see around. I didn't see anybody else, basically. And that was when she had gone to the hospital and had the baby. Of course, I knew she was pregnant like that, she was pregnant. Never gave it a second thought as to whose baby it was, never. Never had that on my mind. It was one of them things where you break up, and 'you go your way, I'll go my way.' So that's how it went, and then shortly after that when they had the baby and all, Ivan came to me and he said, "That's your daughter over there." I'm looking at him like, "What do you mean?" He said, "You better go over there and see her. That's your daughter. You better go see your daughter." That's how he said it: "You just better go see your daughter. That's your daughter." So, I said, "Well, she never told me anything like that was my daughter or anything like that. She never mentioned anything. She got married," or something like that. I said, "I don't have anything to do with this now. She got married and all, and she never mentioned it." Never said anything. So, and then of course, when we were living on Adams

Street, where she had the little efficiency apartment, in the meantime, her brother-in-law Greg, he was staying up there too in the apartment. We were staying over top of them. In my apartment, not her apartment. Because she had the efficiency and I had the regular apartment. And so, later is when I found out that was the brother, her brother, because he always had hot rod cars he worked on in the back there, in the back too, he worked on them, and of course I had a hot rod car at the time. We never really said that much to each other because he done his own thing and I didn't have time because like I say I come from work, I pull my car in there and that was it, we sort of like looked at each other's car. He said he ran the car, he raced it or something like that, and he was always working on it and everything.

He had mentioned to somebody that he didn't think that the baby was his, out on the street or somewhere, whoever it was, I knew that the people who were telling me knew him, of course like I say I didn't know who he was at the time. He came up, something came up a little bit, and I didn't pay too much attention to him.

Yvonne: He said he didn't think that I was his daughter?

Wesley: Yes, because that's the first thing that I mentioned to Yvonne that you had favored ... (*Greg*) That's when the brother came up. (laughs) You favored the brother (*Greg*). Uh-huh. So that's when I had mentioned that to them. I said, "Well, she said the baby looks like his brother Greg." He just looked at me like with those eyes, "Whatever," that's what he looked like. "But I still say that's your daughter." Or something like that, he would say. So, after she told me that and I told her what Ivan had told me, she denied it and said it wasn't my baby, it was his baby. So, I left it alone. That's when it just went on after that. I didn't hear no more from her because like I said she got married and all like that. I didn't bother at that time. And the only time she called me, and of course I kept my same number the whole time too, she called me when you were three years old, two-and-a-half to three I'd say, I would say three. You were a little ole love. You were a little skinny somebody, she

money, and boom, meet you at the back door, whoever came over, a girlfriend or somebody, I met her at the back door, gave her the money and she went on about her business. This was how that went up until you moved over to…what's that place?

Yvonne: New Castle?

Wesley: When do you remember me again?

Yvonne: New Castle.

Wesley: Okay, yeah. I came around there, and you came out.

Yvonne: I was 11.

Wesley: You were 11. You never knew who I was. Said I was Uncle Wesley.

Yvonne: Uncle Wesley.

Wesley: I'd come out there. Your mom would come out, sit in the car and talk. You'd be out there playing. We'd just be sitting in the car talking. And you'd be playing with your cousins or something? Did you have cousins? Because you didn't have no place over there. Did you have cousins over there?

Yvonne: Mm-mm, they weren't cousins.

Wesley: Who were they?

Yvonne: They were just my mom's friend's people.

Wesley: Oh okay, well anyway, okay, that's where I'd come to see you, there. Then of course after you left from there, that's when you went to Brookmont. Yeah, out there. When I was working she called and tell me she was somewhere, because I was living in Odessa then, so she told me to stop by and check on you and stay there until she got home. So that's what I was doing, before I went to Odessa, I'd stop over there and check you out and see what you were doing. I think you were like 13 or 14 then, something like that.

Yvonne: I was 13.

Wesley: Thirteen, okay, so of course I stayed with you and it just went like that. That's how everything went. So, she really didn't admit to me until you were three or four years old, like that. So that's how that went. It was one of them like off and on type things, then of course after that, I took you first to meet Megan, and then Leah. Yeah. And then it was history after that. But yeah, it was something else.

All at the same time, then y'all had that place in Maryland too. Y'all had that place out there with the swimming pool…

Yvonne: In the boondocks?

Wesley: In the boondocks! I mean! She took me out there. I picked her up, she took me out there.

Yvonne: What part of Maryland was that in?

Wesley: Oh man, I don't know. I know it was the boondocks.

Yvonne: Straight boondocks.

Wesley: She got a swimming pool, I don't know did y'all end up swimming in it?

Yvonne: Never.

Wesley: Never, huh?

Yvonne: Never. It was too many rats, rat holes.

Wesley: Well that place was big, but it was just…I don't know what that was all about.

Yvonne: I don't know.

Wesley: But that was the only place I've been other than of course the Elsmere Place, I never did see that one. I know she was there. That's when she had the business and everything. But, she would always call me again, and she would say, she would ask me did I want, she wanted me to go in business with her, her cleaning service or whatever, she wanted me to go in business with her because she was like losing money left and right. He was spending it as fast as she was getting it, or however it was, I guess they both were spending some big bucks, because you got the best of the house, you got some nice places, like I say that Elsmere Place, you were saying it was nice, I never been there.

Yvonne: Oh, you talking about over there by Wilmington High School.

Wesley: Was it? Okay, I never knew where it was.

Yvonne: Was that Els – yeah it had to be. Was it Greenleaf?

Wesley: Yeah, that was the only place I didn't get to see.

Yvonne: That was nice.

Wesley: That's what she said, it was nice.

Yvonne: Mm-hmm.

Wesley: I never did. That's when you all was really into the business then, and I never really mentioned. She kept asking me about the business, and I said not as long as he had a share in the business, I couldn't do that. The only time I'd take the business was if I could take 51%.

Yvonne: After that everything went downhill.

Wesley: It went downhill.

Yvonne: It went downhill.

Wesley: It went downhill. Downhill, man. It's just one of them things where it was like you're on a roller coaster, one of them kind of things. She always kept in touch with me what she was doing, and I always knew, try to keep up with all the kids. (laughs) In the meantime, there was Diane popped in there and along came your other siblings.

<end transcript>

I'm grateful that my relationship with my dad is improving. We are not where we were and not where I believe we are headed. I know that it is the gift of forgiveness that made this possible. I choose to believe that he did the best he could under the circumstances. We are getting to know each other. As long as there is breath, there is opportunity.

I encourage you to waste not another day in unforgiveness. Let go of being right. Let go of being self-righteous. Forgiveness offers you a place of peace, regardless of reconciliation. Go through the process and trust it. You have nothing to lose but the pain.

About the Author

Yvonne Sylvester was born in Wilmington, Delaware. She is the youngest of two on her mother's side and the third born on her father's side. Yvonne lived in Delaware most of her life. Being forced to grow up fast due to abandonment by her parents, wandering was what she knew best. She moved from place to place, lacking stable shelter. As a result, she became a ward of the state at 16 years old and went to live in a group home with her one-year-old son.

She attended various schools throughout the New Castle County area. Among the many schools, she attended Sterck School for the Deaf and Hearing Impaired. Having such a difficult time with stability, she decided that getting her GED was the best route to go and that's what she did. Determined to achieve a childhood goal, she proceeded to attend nursing school. She is currently practicing nursing while attending school to further her education.

Sylvester now has five children, four boys and one girl, whom she raised, giving them the stability that she never had. Three children still reside with her.

Yvonne is adventurous, loves to travel, loves helping people and is industrious. She does not allow her past to dictate her future, forgiving the players in her dark past while forgiving herself in the process. She is inspired to move forward, not looking back or blaming anyone, because after a while, the ball was in her court.

Because of what she has endured, Sylvester made the conscious decision to help others overcome. Knowing what it took for her to forgive and move forward, she has also become a forgiveness coach. Forgiveness coaching is all about helping people get to the place of forgiving themselves and others.

Yvonne Sylvester can be reached for forgiveness coaching, media inquiries, and speaking engagements at 302-883-8817 or info@bloomblossomsoar.com.

www.ingramcontent.com/pod-product-compliance
Lightning Source LLC
Chambersburg PA
CBHW070758100426
42742CB00012B/2187